ROCK AND ROLL MOUNTAINS

ROCK AND ROLL MOUNTAINS

GRAHAM FORBES

MAINSTREAM
PUBLISHING
EDINBURGH AND LONDON

FOR GRAHAM AND ALAN

First published in Great Britain in 2005 by
MAINSTREAM PUBLISHING COMPANY
(EDINBURGH) LTD
7 Albany Street
Edinburgh EH1 3UG

ISBN 1 84018 969 X

A catalogue record for this book is available
from the British Library

Typeset in Badhouse, Circular, Meta and Sabon

Printed in Great Britain by
Antony Rowe Ltd, Chippenham, Wiltshire

AB		MO	
MA		MR	
MB		MT	
MC		MW	
MD			
ME			
MG			
MH			
MM			
MN			

THANKS

Thanks to Alex Mayes, the inspiration, without whom the book would have had a lot of empty pages and I far fewer grey hairs.

I know personal thanks are really cheesy, but I must express my heartfelt gratitude to Bov Allen, Ann McAllister, John McAllister, Nick Webb, Geoff and Kev Sugden, Neil McGeachy, Trudy Fraser, Frances McCartney, Simon Osbourne, Alan Hinkes and all the people over the years, particularly Joan, who have put up with my mood swings, bad temper, awful jokes and various other enchanting habits.

Also thanks to David Fletcher; and Bill Campbell, Deborah Warner, Emily Bland and Lindsay Farquharson at Mainstream for all their help. Special thanks to Dr Andrew Fine at the Sarasota Neurological Unit, Florida, without whose deft use of scalpels and screwdrivers the book would have ended around Chapter 10, but that's another story.

I will also be eternally grateful to Adam, Bill, George, Janet and everyone at Express Removals, Glasgow.

If you want you can
write2g@hotmail.com

CONTENTS

1

ALL OR NOTHING

Marshall stacks and contoured bodies

ALL I WANTED TO DO FROM THE AGE OF 14 WAS PLAY GUITAR IN A BAND.
Any band.

I was convinced that any spotty geek could get laid if he carried a guitar down the street. It didn't matter what kind of guitar: an old Hoffner, a beat-up Burns, a Rosetti – anything with a few rusty strings on it. He didn't even have to be able to play the damn thing, electric guitars just looked so cool, especially the flame-red ones. There was so much exciting music coming out; every morning I woke up and switched on the radio to hear brand-new records by all these fantastic groups with great names – Beatles, Stones, Who, Kinks, Small Faces, Animals, Yardbirds, Pretty Things. London became the city of dreams where you could achieve anything. Everyone felt good, even cats and dogs on the street seemed to be bopping along to the throbbing beat. Boys scrawled the names of their favourite bands in block capitals on their schoolbags and willed their hair to grow, hoping that everyone except their parents and teachers would notice it was hanging over their collars.

Even though his best days were gone, some of the girls in my class at school still liked Elvis. He would have asked their dads' permission for a date; The Beatles would be content to hold their hands, but Mick would have shared them with Keith. The Stones were what rock music was all about.

The Bedford Dormobile was the van of choice for gigging groups in the '60s. Plastered with lipstick messages, it acted as a beacon to thousands of permanently horny schoolboys. When you saw a group's van, your heart pounded: if only you could be like these guys! To have girls – *chicks* – chasing *you* instead of the other way round! I remember seeing The Dominos, or Middle of the Road as they became known, pushing their amplifiers in a couple of old prams along Dumbarton Road in Glasgow to a church-hall dance and even they were surrounded by giggling girls in micro-miniskirts. In every bedroom in Britain, panting teenagers posed with tennis rackets in front of their mirrors, fantasising about being popstars. It was all I thought about.

Although most kids my age wanted to play in groups, almost all of them listened when their fathers shouted at them to get their heads into their schoolbooks and kept it as a dream or a *hobby*. All that singalong shit at parties, strumming a Spanish guitar; those things with nylon strings. No, I wanted to feel the contoured body of a Fender Stratocaster snug against my groin; hear the electric hum and buzz of the jack socket as I plugged the snake-like guitar lead into a huge amplifier at my back; smell the heat of the valves, taste the sweat running down my face, feel the notes screaming and the chords blasting through me into a sea of faces pressed hard against the stage, so close I could touch them.

I believed Mick Jagger when he told us that if we lost our dreams, we would lose our minds. Few of my friends had my lack of foresight, however, and most realised the likely outcome of spending every night of their best years swaying in front of a pile of peeling speaker cabinets blasting out over 100 decibels of power chords and guitar riffs, usually in the keys of E or A – the 'don't fuck with me' keys. Pete Townshend was right; I knew I'd die before I got old. Or at least be stone deaf. I just didn't care. I quit school and spent every spare moment practising guitar. I played with anyone who would have me, anywhere, any time; anything from bowling clubs to Irish showbands.

Then came the '70s. I managed to find a few people as dumb and depraved as me, gave up any semblance of work in the accepted sense and formed a rock band called Powerhouse. No one used the word *group* any more, we were called *bands* now and Ford Transits had become the vans to be seen in. All the local bands used them, rusting heaps bought cheaply at seedy car auctions or from oily builders' yards; death traps with the band's name in white letters stuck to a strip of green film across the top of the windscreen, a clanking padlock and steel bar across the back doors.

We travelled all over Scotland in ours; we called it the Hangover Hotel. If you were ever on the A82 at the time, you will have seen it: a battered old wreck with bare arses smiling at you from the windows. It was skilfully overloaded with Fender guitars, Marshall 4x12s held together with gaffer tape, a ten-piece drum kit, ex-theatre spotlights and all sorts of electrical hazards cunningly packed together in such a way that four hairy, laughing, beer-drinking, belching, farting musos could recline in comfort during the long drives to gigs, and, with a couple of lager-stained mattresses flung over the top of the pile, pull to the side of the road and sleep in it at night.

There were hundreds of gigs. Every little village hall in Scotland had dances at weekends and we loved to play them because the pubs served drink until everyone fell asleep. We also believed that in small communities the farmers' daughters must surely be going insane with pent-up sexual desire – we reckoned they couldn't do it with the local lads or the whole village would know by morning; they'd open their doors at dawn and find queues of grinning youths in their underpants with their tweed trousers neatly folded over their arms, enthusiastically waiting their turn. What more discreet spot to have their first sexual encounter than a mattress in the back of the Hangover Hotel?

The huge, lumbering local lads, all of whom we suspected of being related – the dark clumps of identical eyebrows like prehistoric caterpillars overhanging their faces was what gave it away – did not take kindly to this modern Viking invasion and often we had to leave town, engine roaring, gears screaming. They liked to fight.

Over the years, I had seen plenty of fists and boots flying. I mean, Glasgow is not exactly twinned with Skyros holistic commune, but the worst places of all were little rural communities where the locals knew each other all too intimately and seemed to love head-butting one other at every opportunity. During the week they baled hay together and happily worked side by side, but on Saturday night they were possessed, it seemed, by the forces of mayhem.

The worst place of all was the tranquil island of Islay. Before our gig even started, there were countless brawls: farm lads biting, punching, rolling and gouging, thrashing about all over the village hall. Despite the blood, they never seemed to hurt themselves as they re-enacted the fights they saw on TV. Bruce Lee was obviously a big favourite and occasionally some crazed hyper-boy would climb up on the stage and leap on to the crowd with a scream like a newly neutered cat informing the world of its predicament, his dung-caked Doc Martens seeking out the head of anyone too slow to get out of the way.

We often drove through Glen Coe and I remember lifting my head from endless reams of porn and looking at the mountains towering over us. On one side of the road I could see a long, steep, jagged ridge, like the edge of a saw; on the other, a huge mountain hanging over a little dark loch. Somehow, we got the idea that this pool was as deep as the mountains were high, but a nicely rolled joint could create such notions. The first time I saw the long hump of Ben Nevis from Fort Bill, I had no idea that a couple of years earlier Eric Clapton and his pals in Cream had somehow wandered to the top in an LSD-induced euphoria. All I knew was that the hills looked pretty bloody big.

I often gazed towards the summits of two peaks, watching the sun set behind the high dip between them as though it was a gateway to somewhere, although these romantic notions didn't prevent us annoying English picnickers when we emerged from the Transit in the morning, rubbing the sleep from our eyes as we peed amidst some of the world's most spectacular scenery. We would yawn, stretch and look at ancient lochs and forests, but it never, ever dawned on me that there was a way up these mountains and that people had been climbing them for hundreds of years.

By the age of 21, I was already on more than nodding terms with hash, grass, cocaine, speed, downers, LSD and a few other pills of which I never quite learned the names. When it was available, I enjoyed the mellow dream-like state smoking opium induced – who wouldn't? Somebody once asked Keith Richards if being an addict had worried him. He patiently explained that the whole point of taking heroin is that it makes you incapable of worrying about anything.

Heroin never appealed to me. Only a couple of years after leaving school, when I was living in a little bedsit in Hillhead Street near Glasgow University, I knocked on the door of a room across the hall to bum a cigarette. Inside, eight or nine drooling users sprawled across two single beds, blood trickling down their arms, murmuring and slowly bobbing their heads in time to Pink Floyd's *Atom Heart Mother*. Injecting heroin often made people spectacularly sick, so I had to step over the ever-present puke pails. I never wanted to throw up *that* badly regardless of how wonderful they claimed to feel once they'd barfed and were floating in Sleepy Time.

For musicians, dope was part of the creative process, a tradition handed down by the old Harlem jazzmen, jamming in after-hours clubs, the beatniks of the '50s playing protest songs, and writers like Kerouac and Burroughs, or Huxley tripping in *Brave New World* with his fictional drug 'soma', which sounds very like Ecstasy. Anti-drug campaigners seem unable to grasp that people take these things not because they have problems, but because drugs make them feel good; some people regard Ecstasy as an indispensable part of a good night's clubbing.

The reasons for taking drugs in the '60s and early '70s were different. We took them to expand our awareness, to open up our minds, play the I Ching, talk about philosophy all night, listen to Ginsberg poetry and Bob Dylan. Shagging was pretty good too. We were happy hippies changing the consciousness of the world; hash and marijuana were holy plants, *we didn't touch nothing that our spirits could kill.*

Drugs weren't part of organised crime; gangsters weren't slowly murdering children in every council estate so they could live in luxury Malaga apartments and spiv around in flash cars. You had to be bloody careful, though. In the '60s, Glasgow was full of gangs – they called themselves 'teams'. Media intellectuals often earnestly debated the possible meaning of the war cry 'Tongs Ya Bass'; hey, it was irrelevant when you were sprinting like a hyena on steroids to escape 20 or 30 madmen, out of their minds on cheap wine, as they chased you along Sauchiehall Street, their bayonets cleaving the air.

It was safer, far safer, to be playing guitar in a village hall or peacefully smoking hash in a student flat, than it was to be on the streets at weekends. I saw a wall in the Gorbals on which a gang had painted 'Mental Young Cumbie kick to kill'. It was a simple, unpretentious mission statement that left no room for doubt. If those nutters caught you, you knew what to expect. The genius who came up with that slogan is probably a top ad-agency executive now. Either that or a drug-dealer.

There were one or two oases if you could get there without being head-butted, having your face 'ripped' or your jugular vein slashed by a Stanley knife: a couple of folk clubs (the Incredible String Band had one in Sauchiehall Street – just as the police closed it, Joe Boyd flew to Glasgow from LA and signed them to Electra Records) and also a Friday-night blues club called the Maryland in Scott Street, where you could safely join the hash-heads sitting stoned on the floor and hear great bands like John Mayall, Crusade or Alex Harvey. When Mott the Hoople played there, I got talking to Ian Hunter and he told me, 'A lot of rock stars may look stoned, but they sure as hell weren't when they put their bands together.'

I took his advice and immediately stopped taking drugs; not everyone can have an immune system like Lemmy from Motorhead. I was desperate to make it in the music business. It was all I thought about. *I could sleep at night as a rock and roll star.*

2

GOOD TIMES BAD TIMES

On the road with the ISB

WHEN I LANDED LUCKY AT 23 AND MANAGED TO SMOOTH-TALK MY WAY INTO A well-paid, world-touring gig with the Incredible String Band, it was a dream come true. The band had originally been an eclectic folk group, the first to play what is now called 'world music'. It had a massive following, had played Woodstock – the only Scots band to do so – and had even been the first British band to play in Spain under Franco. The group's early albums had been huge, only The Beatles, Stones and The Who sold more in the late '60s.

Mike Heron, one of the band's founders, had made a solo album with Pete Townshend and Keith Moon playing on it, and on a trip to London I met Mike by chance and immediately offered my band, Powerhouse, as backing on his next one. I'd never lacked nerve. Mike invited me to his cottage in the Scottish Borders where he handed me an expensive reel-to-reel tape recorder and told me to figure out guitar parts to various new songs he had written. After I'd finished, I went back to Glasgow and the pub-and-club circuit. A week later, Mike called. He asked me to come back again and introduced me to a bass player and drummer, and told us to play; it was to be recorded in his little studio next door. After a couple of hours' jamming, he told me the String Band were going to be playing less acoustic music, that he'd always loved rock, and the band were about to go on tour with a load of new material. He was looking for a rock guitarist. He'd let me know.

All the way back to Glasgow I was shaking. It had never occurred to me that I had been auditioning for one of the most successful bands in the world. I didn't sleep or stray more than an arm's length from the telephone for the next three days. Less than two weeks later, I was staring down at the English Channel from a plane as we headed to France for the start of a huge tour.

When we flew over the Alps heading to do a TV show in Italy, I saw more soaring mountains, even bigger than the ones in Glen Coe. I am certain I saw climbers look up from the snow on some jagged summit and wave at the plane, but it never occurred to me that ordinary people could do that. I had plenty of other things to occupy my attention: playing in the band required a lot of concentration. At first, some of the older fans were stunned to hear the new songs, but the more gigs we played, the more we attracted younger audiences and the band gained thousands of new followers. It was a lot of fun.

One fairly typical night, halfway through a European tour, was when we played in Naples. One of our road crew, Geoff, had got talking to two local girls and arranged to meet them after the gig. They were very attractive, scantily dressed – half naked, in fact, which was always a good sign – and more than happy to take Geoff and me down to the town square to sample the delights of the city, which we guessed might include them in half an hour or so. All of a sudden, a car pulled up, three plain-clothes cops leapt out and began shouting at us. When they realised we were foreigners, they yelled at the girls; thought they were hookers. I suppose they were a bit raunchy – you could see at a glance they weren't saving themselves for Mr Right. It was the bare stomachs, braless crop-tops, tiny leather skirts and fishnet stockings that did it, I guess. They were spot on . . . the sort of girls you wouldn't invite home for Christmas dinner. The police were agitated about something and Geoff asked the girls what was going on.

'They say is just routine check. They want to know who you are, to see your passports.'

We told them we didn't have them with us. They weren't amused.

'We must go with them to hotel to see your passports.'

I fumbled through my pockets until I found a brochure for the one we were staying at – it was the only way I could ever remember – then we all piled into their car and they drove towards the Intercontinental or whatever it was called. As we neared the entrance, the driver put his foot down and the car shot off, bouncing along the backstreets. Geoff and I had finished off a bottle of the dressing-room vino after the gig and were relaxed about the whole thing; it would be a laugh telling the rest of the band in the morning. Finally, the car screeched to a halt outside a dark doorway and we were led up a stone staircase into a dimly lit room with a few wooden chairs and a long oak table.

One of the cops spoke halting English and told Geoff and me to write down our names and addresses. We duly obliged: Andy Capp, 69 Blowjob Street, Manchester; Harold Steptoe, 2 Upyourarse Avenue, Kent. The cop nodded grimly, put the paper in a drawer, then started yelling at the girls. I lost my temper and shouted at him: what the fuck did he think he was doing bringing us here? We're British . . . what right did he have to harass us like this?

He took off his jacket, sneered and patted the biggest gun I have ever seen. *Shit*. I guess that gave him the right. That's all we needed, a *Dirty Harry* fan. His hand-cannon said it clearly, *sit down and shut the fuck up*. So I did. The cops looked through the girls' bags, then told us all to piss off, *va funculo* or something. When we got back out to the street, I asked one of the girls why the cops had hassled us.

'They thought we had drugs,' she said, clearly shaking.

'Fuck's sake . . . just as well you didn't,' I said, 'we've got a tour to do. Don't fancy spending the next ten years in one of your jails.' I could just hear that lonesome whistle blow.

The girls looked at each other, their faces pale. 'Eh . . . we have.' One of them reached into her bag and pulled out a lump of hash; somehow the cop had missed it.

'Jesus Christ, get rid of it. Throw it down a drain!'

There is no doubt about it, touring with a band is never boring.

We had just finished a hugely successful three-month tour of America when it all went sour. We had signed to an American record company who loved the new music we were playing; they were convinced we could move away from being a cult-status band and break into the mainstream markets dominated by FM radio. This had horrified the other founder member, Robin Williamson, and he and Mike stayed on in New York after the tour to discuss the contract, trying to find some compromise.

We had huge tours of the US, New Zealand, Australia and Europe booked, and things were looking good. Mike and Robin met in the Mayflower Hotel in a suite overlooking Central Park, began screaming at each other and vowed never to work together again. I was back in Glasgow, resting after the tour at the flat of my girlfriend, Joan, when Mike called and asked me to help put a new band together. I immediately flew to London to meet him, then, with the String Band drummer, John Gilston, trawled the Marquee, Dingwalls and other clubs until we found a good keyboard player and bass player. Mike was writing some great stuff, in a style like a British Bruce Springsteen. I was very disappointed that the ISB had fallen apart, especially as we had been doing so well, but loved touring with Mike's new band, who were all great players. Unfortunately, it didn't last.

We recorded an album and did a British tour, the John Peel show . . . the usual sorts of things, and were about to go to the

States where we planned to base ourselves for the next year when the American company we were signed to hit financial troubles and starved us of the cash we needed to stay on the road. Using his own money, Mike kept the band going as best he could, but it was very difficult. We returned from a fantastic sold-out tour of Holland and realised we couldn't do any more gigs without record-company backing; the costs were too high.

The only time I felt at home was when I was on a stage; playing gigs in London was fantastic, but sitting around my hotel room wasn't. The band was gradually grinding to a standstill and I didn't know what to do at night. The guys in the band all lived miles apart, but there were plenty of lively pubs nearby . . .

We took wage cuts, but it was expensive living in London; we ran up bank overdrafts and kept rehearsing every day, hoping things would soon be sorted, but the atmosphere in the band was becoming more and more tense. We couldn't sign with anyone else until the legal mess that came with being contracted to a dying record label was resolved. One day I came to the rehearsal studio hung over and irritable, and after playing songs we'd gone over 100 times before, Mike and I fell out and he sacked me. Even though it had been the only row we'd ever had, and we are still close friends, it was over.

I always had the discipline not to drink during gigs, but afterwards . . . drinking yourself stupid every night and getting up to all sorts of escapades was just the normal rock 'n' roll lifestyle; it was what rock guitarists *did*. I stayed in London for a while afterwards and was offered auditions with Manfred Mann and other bands, but eventually decided to go back to Glasgow. I felt like playing with my pals again; they knew how to have a good time, which at that moment, was all I wanted.

3

WHAT MADE MILWAUKEE FAMOUS

The drink

I WAS BACK IN SCOTLAND, PLAYING WITH MY OLD BAND POWERHOUSE AT THE US Navy base at Dunoon and the boys from the dry dock were screaming their war cry, enjoying their usual riotous Saturday night. *Chew tobacca, chew tobacca, chew tobacca, Spit! If you ain't the dry dock, then you ain't shit!* None of these guys had been at the front of the line at Uncle Sam's recruitment office in Times Square, washed and polished and armed with an eager, quivering salute. They were reluctant conscripts – they had all been caught committing minor crimes and had been given the choice of two years in jail or the same time in the navy. Since none of them fancied having their butts permanently stretched in a federal penitentiary, they'd ended up in Scotland. It was no vacation: their commanding officer saw to it that they spent their sentences scrubbing crap off the hulls of nuclear subs. When their weekly night off rolled round, they raised hell in the Enlisted Men's Club. If they liked you, the atmosphere was great.

The base was officially on American soil and everything had

been done to create a home-town feel. We were popular because we made a lot of noise playing stuff like 'Sweet Home Alabama'. You didn't dare not to. The dry-dockers loved Lynyrd Skynyrd and would join in, singing, *Lord, I'm comin' home to you*, stamp their feet, jump on the tables, yell out their chant and grind against the ageing hookers they'd imported from downtown Dunoon. *Hey, play a slow dance, buddy, I'm HOT.*

Sometimes, I wondered what the hell I was doing back here – a year earlier in London, when I was playing with Mike, I'd jammed with Leon Wilkeson, Skynyrd's bass player – but then I'd throw back a tequila, drink another beer and forget about it. The dry-dockers bought Buds for us by the caseload, which was very helpful since visiting bands were prohibited from buying alcohol.

As soon as we finished the gig, we heard the sound of another group playing at the nearby officers' mess. Someone told us it was an all-girl band and we were off like a shot. It took us ten seconds to convince the crew-cut guards at the door that we were their roadies and we were inside. It was a formal affair, long dresses and restrained dancing on a shining French-chalked, polished oak floor, a complete contrast to the yelling, denim-clad, drunken crazies to whom we'd been playing. We took one look at the five beautiful girls onstage playing Carpenters and Abba hits and knew we had found love. For that night anyway. We couldn't wait until they'd finished. We spread around the elegant room, slurping down any unattended glasses we found on the tables. There were plenty: brandy, wine, whisky, some champagne. Tasty.

We were getting a little peckish – it had been a four-hour gig, after all – when we spotted it: a huge cake, beautifully crafted to look like a golf course with little marzipan golfers, green icing, cream, frosted-sugar bunkers. It looked fantastic. There was a plaque at the front, saying something about a link between the US Navy Officers' Club and the Royal & Ancient at St Andrews. Evidently, it was to be cut in some sort of ceremony, and it basked on a large stand under the glow of sensitively arranged spotlights.

We wanted something to eat, so I lurched out to the Transit, which we'd parked in a building site outside, and came back with a rusty old spade, staggered to the little podium, then, before anyone could stop me, rammed it into the cake and calmly walked back to the van with the top layer teetering on the shovel. As I lurched out, there was a stunned silence, broken only by the band laughing themselves silly. I looked over my shoulder and saw a distinguished man in an immaculate dinner suit staring at me with a look of horror. It was Prince Philip.

The drink. It's a terrible thing, as they say in Glasgow.

I was drinking a lot.

I was heavily in debt to the taxman and the bank, but somehow any money I made ended up in the cash register of the nearest bar. I am embarrassingly slow on the uptake about a lot of things, but I was beginning to realise that I had a serious weakness and, like so many Scots before me, I was one of those people who simply could not touch the stuff.

I had friends, seen-and-done-it-all musicians, who regularly finished off a night's drinking by gulping down Old Spice or dental mouthwash – anything that was more than 0.5 per cent proof, and I figured that I was fine, I'd never get to *that* state. I was 27, had gone from headline tours, playing the big stages of Europe and America, back to greasy, smoke-filled social clubs, churning out country and western tunes to keep me in ready cash for my daily treks to the off-licence. Instead of living in luxury hotels and Chelsea apartments, I was holed up in a shitty little low-rent, cold-water, room-and-kitchen basement flat. The old guy across the dark, urine-stinking corridor cleaned buses at night; as soon as he clocked off, he drank until he crawled home and I usually had to step over him where he lay unconscious in a pool of vomit and piss.

It was fucking embarrassing.

When anyone asked why I was back in Glasgow and what I was doing these days, I just mumbled whatever came to mind. I didn't know, except that I needed a nightly intake of alcohol. Soon, even playing guitar became too much hassle. Terrible thing, *the drink.*

I had few career options: my erratic mood swings made me virtually unemployable and, anyway, I had no recognised skills unless you count being able to change a set of guitar strings in under nine minutes. Perhaps I wasn't looking hard enough, but I don't recall seeing any ads in employment-agency windows along the lines of: 'Urgently needed: hung over guitarist, ability to get out of bed before 11 a.m. an advantage, but not essential.'

After I'd come back to Glasgow, I had done some writing, if that's what you'd call sending glowing reviews of Powerhouse's pub gigs to the music press – under a false name, of course. I'd even written a novel about the music business that a publisher had thought promising, although not quite compatible with their list. In other words, it was shite. I could see their point: the half I'd written when I was sober was fine, the rest read like it had been scrawled in an asylum. They asked me to try something else and I sent off a couple of chapters. This was exactly what they were looking for. Great; any chance of a modest advance? Sorry, no. I would have to send them two more chapters. I really intended to write those extra words, but something happened that got in the way of my troubling the editors any further.

Desperate for money, I started a business with Mickey, the drummer with Powerhouse, another lost soul who, like me, had a permanent ringing noise in his ears. It was just a little trucking business – nothing fancy, you realise. I had a pal who owned a junk shop and needed wardrobes, dressing tables and cheap paraffin heaters delivered to damp bedsits that were in many of the old tenements in the West End. The great thing was that he would pay us cash every day. I borrowed £100 from a guy in the pub and bought a beat-up little van. Years of packing glass-valved amplifiers into Transits had not been entirely wasted.

I hadn't intended it to be a long-term career. I just wanted to get my overdraft down to a few figures, get the Inland Revenue off my case – they were taking my outstanding tax way too seriously – and tear the ring-pulls off a fresh pile of foaming cans every night. I'd shift furniture for a while, then maybe move back to London and join a decent band.

It was depressing to see albums I had played on in some of the flats where I was lugging crappy pre-war furniture, but most days Mickey and I enjoyed it. The first couple of deliveries sweated out the morning hangover. By one o'clock, we were ravenous and knew a little diner that served real burgers with soft poached eggs on top, just the way we liked them. Then we'd double-park outside the auction rooms – there was always someone who had bought an antique sideboard too big to fit into their estate car. Twenty pounds, please.

At the end of every day, we poured some gas in the tank, divided the cash and swanned through the pub doors like Southern plantation owners. I had a great feeling of freedom; I wasn't dependent on some record company. We could pay the rent, eat and have money left to fold into our pockets; we didn't give a fat rat's ass about anything. Best of all, we didn't have to spend our nights backing awful cabaret singers or playing 'Show Me the Way to Amarillo' to drunks dancing the 'slosh' in East Butthump Miners' Club. We could get happily pissed, even drink ourselves unconscious, whenever we wanted.

But I knew I couldn't go on like that. There was no chance of me going to AA. I mean, come on, I know they have helped countless thousands, but at my age the last thing I wanted to do was sit around with a bunch of red-nosed, twitching old farts whining about their lost lives. I knew this was my last chance and if I blew it now, it was over. *Nobody knows you when you're down and out.*

I had done some dumb things when I had been drinking. I mean *really* dumb. Shit, more than 20 years later, I still have cold sweats just thinking about some of my deeds of utterly incomprehensible stupidity: the hotel parties that had got a little out of hand; the rooms that had been left looking like an explosion in a furniture factory; the wardrobe I'd heaved out of a sixth-floor window into an Amsterdam canal; the planes I'd almost missed on tour because I'd gone off with wild women to their apartments and forgotten where the hell I was; the night I only *just* avoided being arrested in Tennessee by a stunned traffic cop who had never seen a Scotsman sitting *outside* a car, arse in the window, hanging on to the roof as it raced along the freeway at two in the morning with three beautiful groupies and a stoned roadie inside laughing so hard they wet themselves. Then there was *that* night in New York, or the one in Brussels . . . There had been so many . . . *the drink*.

Humping furniture around could provide a decent, if unglamorous, living, at least for the time being, but I had to get out of bed with a clear head in the morning at more or less the same time as the rest of the workaday world. I would have to quit drinking.

Long-suffering Joan and I married and a year later had Graham, the first of our two sons. For the next few years, I managed to stay away from the bars during the week, but at weekends – *honest, I'm only going out for a few beers* – I always ended up lurching home like someone lost in a blizzard. One Saturday morning, I woke with Graham tugging at the duvet. He wanted to play something noisy with me, but I had yet another head-crushing hangover. I heard my crabbit voice barking at him and when I saw the hurt look in his eyes, I'd never felt so low.

This shit has got to stop.

4

BORN UNDER A BAD SIGN

Wee Jake and the Mutants

I HAD TO FIND SOMETHING TO DO AT WEEKENDS THAT WOULD GET ME AWAY from whoever was buying the next round. In Glasgow, if you tell someone you don't drink, they stare in bewilderment as though you have some rare disease. It's just not *normal*.

I started thinking about the mountains I'd seen when we had driven to gigs. You'd think that mountains would be to Scots what surf was to The Beach Boys, or snow is to Norwegians. You can see the outer edges of the Highlands – an area as spectacular as the Alps – from Glasgow and Edinburgh. I'd grown up in a country with hundreds of the most beautiful mountains in the world, but at school we were never taught about them, even though Scotland is the birthplace of mountaineering. I remember my head dropping on to my chest during endless lessons on Lord Nelson and Napoleon, but never being told about John Muir, the Scottish explorer and father of conservation, who has all sorts of American national parks and stuff named after him. We were taught more about the wheatfields of Canada (bloody hell, nobody could make *that* interesting) than the Highlands of our own country. Although I grew up in Glasgow, I'd never noticed I was surrounded by hills.

So I decided I'd go and have a look. Why not? But would I be fit enough? When I was at school, I was pretty much hopeless at sport. I always wanted to be picked for the school team, had wanted it so badly: dreamed of running into the penalty box, leaving huge, bloodthirsty defenders sprawled in the mud, then lobbing the ball over the goalkeeper's head. I just didn't have the strength, balance or skill.

This hasn't improved as I've grown older. I often lurch into startled shoppers in department stores when the floor surface changes from carpet to vinyl – surely I'm not the only one who does that? – I have even fallen on my face for no obvious reason, to anyone else that is. My mind leaps from one idea to another in a totally random way and I'm always trying to do two things at once, like walk in different directions. It's simple really, I understand it – I am not an athlete. I've accepted it and, thankfully, so have my friends when I veer into them for no apparent reason. I just can't walk in a straight line. I don't mean this in a Bill Bryson sort of way. I know that many writers copy him and think they too are amusing by portraying themselves as happily hapless; I am just being honest. With a guitar in my hands, I am fine; without one, I am just tall and gangly and uncoordinated.

I was also smoking far too many cigarettes; it was time to quit, especially now that I had a son and Joan was expecting our second; there is nothing worse than hearing a baby with a 40-a-day cough. I decided I should go to a gym or something, but, at that time, the only clubs nearby were for serious weightlifters. No, thanks. Carrying sideboards and dusty old pianos was enough. I thought I'd try swimming. Someone told me that Glasgow University had a really good pool at the Stevenson Building on Oakfield Avenue, so I called them, but there was no chance of being allowed in unless I was a student. None whatsoever. Sorry, absolutely no exceptions. Pity.

When I had been touring with the String Band and Mike Heron, I had learned how to talk my way backstage at most places and had met Bruce Springsteen, Bonnie Raitt, Steve Stills, Rod Stewart . . . even spent a night on the piss with Julie Christie when she was filming in Nashville, although her bodyguard kept a very close watch on me. How hard could it be to get into a bloody swimming pool? I went and had a look. They were very careful about keeping out anyone who shouldn't have been there. Security gates, photo IDs, loads of staff on duty, the whole thing. After about ten minutes, I figured out how to get in and then went regularly, which helped get rid of a few of the pounds that drinking had piled on. Eventually, I got to know the managers and when I told them I had been using the place, they were baffled, especially when I mentioned I never paid; just walked in and out whenever I felt like it. They reckoned it was impossible. They reviewed all their security systems and couldn't figure it out. After a couple of weeks, I showed them how it was done and they let me buy an annual membership.

As always with gatecrashing, it was simple. I had noticed that students would come out of the building, go for a jog, then return to complete their workout. Wearing shorts and a towel round my neck, I jogged right in with them. The security staff always assumed I'd signed in earlier and I would give them a friendly nod as I walked by them, panting a little for effect. After a couple of months, I soon felt ready to try climbing a hill.

But who would I go with? The only people I'd ever known who wandered around mountains had wholesome appetites, rosy cheeks, plump arses (but firm muscles) and *never* swore. At school, they had been the stalwarts of the Scripture Union, collected stamps and carefully built towering cranes from Meccano. They *enjoyed* playing rugby. They went to university and studied useful things like engineering. They were the khaki-shorts brigade: healthy, jovial characters who marched off to campsites every weekend and sang drinking songs around the campfire. No thanks.

So I called Jake.

'Wee' Jake had been a shit-hot bass guitarist I'd played beside during hundreds of booze-fuelled gigs. By now, he'd realised he was an alcoholic. It is very difficult to quit *the drink*. People with far more going for them – beautiful wives, children, careers, homes, money, everything – have ended up pissing it all away. We all know this and we all know a few. Jake was another of life's casualties; he was doomed from the moment he first stepped inside his local pub, felt the warmth embrace him and the tension so easily vanish after a few glasses of Islay gold. When the love of his life left him after he blew yet another week's rent on whisky, there could be no other outcome. It is very sad, but there it is.

When Wee Jake was sober, he was painfully shy. *The drink* made him extrovert, but just a little too blunt with people. He would get blootered, then blurt out whatever came into his head; he sounded like someone with Tourette's on sodium pentathol. Glasgow is not the place for unrestrained frankness and he frequently spent nights in casualty wards. He was not a fighter – he was thin, and lived on beans and toast and tinned soup – and a strong wind could have blown him over. He knew where it would all end, but he was powerless to resist, like someone being sucked out of an aeroplane. One night, he had staggered into a packed pub in Partick where a screaming mob was watching the last, tense minutes of a crucial Scotland World Cup match on a big-screen television. For some reason, he'd uttered a manic laugh, then ripped the mains cable clean off the plug . . .

Jake had long since pawned his bass and was resigned to a life on the dole – he'd even managed to get the girl at the desk to stamp that discreet little red mark on his signing-on card, signifying that he wasn't quite right in the head, so the staff wouldn't pressurise him to attend job interviews. I only recognised it because I used to have one too.

He'd found himself a little bedsit and, by doing odd jobs about the place, the landlord often waived his rent. Jake had decided he wouldn't even think about finding a proper job, he reckoned there was no point: he usually only lasted until the first pay day before vanishing on one of his binges. He knew the more he earned, the more he drank; in the strange world of Jake-logic, not working was his way of keeping his drinking under control.

He was so timid that he could never speak to girls unless he was incoherently drunk, even though he was a good-looking little guy; the girls at gigs loved him with his shy baby-face and long, blond hair. If he'd been willing to make the trip to Queensborough Terrace in Bayswater to have intimate, eh, career talks with Jonathan King, he might have got a gig with one of those '70s pop bands, like another bass player I knew. He was so young-looking that even when he was 30, pubs asked him for ID. Those that hadn't already barred him, that is.

He'd met two sisters who were absolute monsters, into everything illegal: shoplifting, breaking into cars, burglary, whatever they could get away with; small-time drug-dealers buying prescription temazepam cheap from pensioners and reselling it to the jelly addicts – nothing was beyond their repertoire. They were small, with high wobbling arses, podgy arms and little stumpy legs. Jake called them the Mutants.

They hated everyone and their neighbours would have nothing to do with them. Their sneering faces were active volcanoes of pus and snot, and their stubby hands were always clutching a can of super-strength lager. They slouched on street corners, hoovering slime from depositories in their deepest nasal cavities, hawking and snorting mucus into their mouths, then gobbing lumps of greasy phlegm on to the street, muttering to themselves and swearing at anyone who passed. If they had not been so easily identifiable, they would happily have robbed little children and mugged old ladies collecting their last pension cheques; they would show no mercy.

Every other Tuesday, when he cashed his benefit cheque, Jake lurched from the pub, bounced off parked cars and banged on the door of the Mutants' dark basement flat; it was not the most romantic of arrangements. He was desperately lonely, still haunted by the memory of his lost love, but once he'd been at *the drink* . . .

I thought if we got some fresh air, maybe walked up one of the hills near Glasgow, it might help both of us quit *the drink*. It was worth a try. I persuaded him to come for a walk to see the interestingly named Whangie, a weird little rock canyon at the top of a gentle hill about 20 minutes from the smoky bars of Byres Road. His hands were shaking. It was 24 hours until giro day and he was desperate for a cigarette and a swally, as he called it; I promised him both if he came along. That swung it. I hoped this would be a turning point for him.

We drove to the Queen's View car park, a well-known nocturnal shagging-spot at the foot of the hill, and began walking to the top. It was a beautiful July day and the sun was warm on our backs. I looked at Jake and was rewarded with a smile; he was enjoying this. He strode up, admiring the view, enjoying the sweat dripping from his face, laughing that if it wasn't for the sheuch – the channel – of his arse, he'd drown. His sweat had the sweet, acidic smell of alcohol; this was doing him the world of good. Then he noticed some sheep further up and eyed them with suspicion. Suddenly, he froze.

'What kind of animals do you get up here?'

I'd no idea, but started listing the obvious makes, like foxes and hares and rabbits, those brands. I'd never been a David Attenborough fan, except for that documentary where killer whales, like aquatic basketball players, lob unlucky seals in the air.

'But no snakes, eh? You don't get snakes in Scotland, do you?' He peered into the long grass at his feet.

'Well, maybe. Yeah, I suppose . . . maybe adders . . . nothing . . .'

In a nanosecond, he'd whipped round and was running downhill to the car, rolling and tumbling, his eyes wide, glaring at the ground as if he wished he didn't have to put his feet on it.

'Jesus Christ . . . snakes . . . There's fucking snakes in that fucking grass . . . fucking hell . . . snakes, for fuck's sake . . .'

He never went near a hill again. But he did find a nice girlfriend.

5

I CAN SEE FOR MILES

Duncryne Hill

IT WAS A FEW YEARS BEFORE I HAD TIME TO TRY HILLWALKING AGAIN. UNLESS you are used to clawing open your eyes every morning and groaning, regretting how much you drank and whatever else you did last night, swearing tonight will be different and knowing with a sick feeling in your stomach that it won't, then having to swallow a pint of water with codeine and suck down several lungfuls of smoke before you can move a bloody inch, you can't fully appreciate how wonderful it feels to greet the day with a clear head. In one of these euphoric moments of clarity, I had decided that instead of farting around delivering old wardrobes, it would be easy to build a proper removal company. I could eventually employ a manager to run it and get back to playing. Hell, why not?

I borrowed what seemed a huge amount of money and bought my first proper moving van. Mickey threw up his hands. He loved driving the huge truck on the motorway and the roar of the six-cylinder diesel engine throbbing under his arse (especially when he was sitting just behind the bumper of some dozy pillock hogging the middle lane at 30 mph), but he couldn't keep down his nightly prawn madras – the drummer's delight – through worrying about getting deep into debt. He asked if I would be willing to employ him as a driver and pay him a weekly wage; he really didn't want to be involved in running a business. Had I guessed what the next ten years would be like, I would have torn up the loan forms there and then.

I spent most of my time finding customers; Mickey drove the van and he went back to playing in club bands at weekends. He was still drinking for five hours every night, but was so easygoing it never worried him. He was a drummer, after all. Besides, he never seemed to suffer from ferocious hangovers and, unlike me, when he was drunk, he only rarely underwent complete personality shifts and became a one-man disaster area.

With the caution that had been the hallmark of my life, I rushed headlong into buying more trucks which involved employing removal men. Lots of them. Nowadays, the industry is much more professional, but it was different then – you tended to be suspicious of men who claimed they never touched a drop; there was usually a dark reason, like they'd committed murder or something. I took on many guys who had problems with *the drink*, but never let the fact that they might be alcoholics deter me from giving them a job – I couldn't really, considering my life up to that point – as long as they didn't touch it while they were working. Some of them took a lot of watching; they were fine until a bottle reached their mouths, then they changed completely. I understood only too well.

'Tam the Bam' was a terrific driver and as conscientious a worker as you would ever hope to find. He was mild-mannered, honest, polite, and doted on his wife and young kids at home in the huge graffiti-covered council estate where he lived. An English catalogue company gave credit to people like Tam – those who had been refused it by everyone else – but at crippling interest rates, of course. He'd placed an order for expensive beech bedroom furniture and his wife called to say that it had been delivered. It was Friday and he'd stopped at the pub on the way home. He had stayed a little too long and his wife let him know it when he staggered into the house. Less than five minutes later, the brand-new wardrobes, chests of drawers, bedside cabinets – the lot – had been reduced to shrapnel. They hadn't even made the first payment on their five-year loan.

Just around the corner lived 'Flipper' (a van had once run over his foot), who had ordered 96 cans of super-strong lager in nice time for Christmas. He had calculated that they would last him at least a week. His neighbours saw them being carried into his flat and were at his door in an instant, shaking his hand, wishing him the compliments of the season. A couple of hours later, Flipper was left with 96 empty cans to put in the dustbin and a year of monthly payments to the catalogue company.

'Hey Broon!' was another terrific old-style moving man who could wrap furniture beautifully. He used to sit quietly in a corner by himself smoking a roll-up until he was called to help carry something. *Hey Broon!* Too many nights ended the same way for him: he'd drink until there was nothing left. He decided to change his ways and ordered a bike from the catalogue company; it would be healthy cycling to work. The night it was delivered, he took it for a test run to the Old Bench Bar, which was, in fact, an old bench standing amid weeds, discarded tyres and oil cans on a long-abandoned dock at the side of the River Clyde. He'd joined some of his mates who were enjoying their usual Friday-evening 'aire libre' wine-tasting. They weren't too concerned about vintage, nose and body, or whether it had a fruity aftertaste, the usual Buckfast and Eldorado did them fine. It was a hot summer night and they were refreshed out of their minds. Hey Broon! soon caught up. For some reason that I could never quite understand, they were teasing him about the bike, something about him entering the Tour de France, and so he lobbed it into the oily depths of the Clyde. He was still making payments two years later.

Another guy who worked for me had a lucid, highly intelligent mind that, unfortunately, was all too often clouded by dark moods. He could have succeeded at many things, but none of them entailed drinking every night to the point that his legs became like springs, barely able to carry him home. He also bought a mail-order bike, but got the size wrong and a child's model was delivered. He couldn't be bothered sending it back and used it anyway, looking very strange cycling beside the thundering Clydeside Expressway with his knees sticking out at right angles like Coco the Clown.

He was a troubled soul; you never knew when darkness would descend on him like a lead overcoat. I knew exactly how he felt, but I had woken up to the fact that, although I had a mind like an out-of-control firework display, I could somehow pass myself off as a normal human being and keep a roof over my kids' heads and Nikes on their feet – provided I stayed away from *the drink*, not just during the week, but permanently.

I loved spending any spare time I had with my young sons, taking them out to the country to enjoy the fresh air while they were at an age when they could be talked into such things. It made a change from our usual game of belching as loud as humanly possible at Burger King, although that was great fun too. A little hillwalking might be just the thing.

I bought a very helpful little guidebook by a guy called Gilbert Summers and we set off to Gartocharn, a little village I had plundered with Powerhouse years before, then wandered up a nearby hill called Duncryne. When we stepped onto the top, my eyes shot open like satellite dishes. Although it was only a small hill, it stood alone above flat fields and so it was almost like looking down from a plane. Loch Lomond stretched away from us and we could see large mountains towering over the still, deep water. The only sound was of birds, or perhaps the quiet clatter of a distant tractor and the gentle purring of a vet's car as he drove to tend a lamb somewhere. The loch was as calm as the Dalai Lama.

A humped little mountain called Conic Hill dipped down to the water like a thirsty dinosaur and a row of small islands continued from its base across the loch. This is, the book said, the line that separates the Lowlands and the Highlands. I had never really thought about it. I had always assumed that the Highlands was simply the bit above Stirling – 'up north'. When we had done gigs in little villages there, we'd driven, eh, up the way to get to them. But, according to the book, it is not a simple geographic difference.

Apart from having all the big mountains (which is a pretty obvious difference, even to me), the Highlands has a different geological formation to the Lowlands; the composition of the rock is not the same. The reason is exciting – well, it is to me. The two regions were actually different continents until 450 million years ago when they collided with what must have been one hell of a bang, throwing up huge mountains on one side. There are mountains in Torridon, in the north-west Highlands, that are the oldest in the world. Some have been around for over 2,500 million years, far longer than Everest.

The dividing line between the two areas is a fault zone – like the San Andreas in California – that starts way out in the deep Atlantic and cuts diagonally across Scotland through Arran to Stonehaven. Called the Highland Boundary Fault, there are frequent vibrations along its length, though they are quite mild, as these things go, measuring less than four on the Richter scale – enough to shake the plates off the walls. Could there ever be a San Francisco-style earthquake in Scotland? Yes, according to geologists.

Looking northwards from Duncryne, I could see countless soaring mountains. It dawned on me that if I could haul my arse up here without my heart exploding, there might be easy ways up those hills too. They were sitting there just waiting for me, and walking tired me out enough to sleep at night without getting jittery for a two-hour nightcap at the nearest bar. I took a deep breath. Perhaps this could help me calm down a little; my mind was always like a damn war zone. I stood staring at the entrance to this great natural arena and couldn't take my eyes off it.

It was just so perfect.

6

PILGRIM

Western sunsets

SOMEHOW, FURNITURE DELIVERIES AND REMOVALS WERE PAYING THE BILLS. I found it hard to believe that I was suddenly longing to do hills and not five-piece female bands. I was becoming hooked on something healthy for a change. And safe – or so I reckoned.

I am more than a little compulsive, so I bought piles of books on hillwalking and climbing, but they were awful. Most were as predictable as a Mills and Boon, but without the sweaty sex. Strong-jawed mountaineers droning on about shouldering rucksacks, dodging avalanches, fighting their way to some desperate summit or other, affecting a ludicrously casual attitude to the danger they faced. The books were riddled with gung-ho statements like, 'It was good to be climbing vertical rock again,' leading to, 'This was getting serious.' Then, finally, 'As I fell, the mountain crashed by my face in a blur. I waited for the inevitable crack of my bones shattering and hoped that the end would be swift.'

Yeah, right.

Any account of *knowingly* plummeting to your death that

does not start with 'the instant I fell, the entire contents of my bowels exploded into my underpants' is a load of old bollocks. I just don't believe it. And, anyway, all I wanted to do was get some fresh air and maybe catch a nice view.

I looked around for a book that might be a bit less macho and found a biography in which an American climber describes in painstaking detail every nuance of her formative years, each weary mile of her expeds, every bloody tedious ascent she has ever done: '. . . I managed to hand-jam a tiny crack – being female has its advantages – then curled my fingers over a crimp-hold . . .' Yawn. She regales us with full details of her wonderful, perfect kids and their life achievements. Hell, she even tells us about her first period. Like we care. What we all wanted to know was this: what did her husband back home think about her sharing a tent for weeks on end with her young, healthy male climbing partner and, specifically, what exactly did they do to while away those long, boring Alaskan nights? Are you really telling us that in the cold of your frost-covered tent, the silence broken only by the crash of an all-too-near avalanche, a hand didn't stretch out in the dark for a little comfort? An arm, a simple hug – for warmth perhaps? We would understand.

Even some of the better biographies are written like the Boy Scout annual with those cringeworthy little character descriptions of steadfast mountaineers. You know the sort of thing: 'Tall, with tousled hair, a ready wit and winning smile, yet staunch in the face of adversity, Reginald was just the chap to have at your side when seracs were toppling and the chips were down.' Tell the truth, for fuck's sake. You like sharing a tent with him because he doesn't snore, always farts outside (except after curries) and only jerks off once a week.

Of the pile of books I read, one was different; a beautifully written story of Scottish climbing in the 1930s by Alastair Borthwick called *Always A Little Further*. It avoids all the jaunty tales of high-altitude bullshit. It makes Scotland sound wonderful – just the place to calm jangling nerves instead of drowning them in tequila.

In Gilbert Summers' guidebook, I found clear descriptions of routes up impressive mini-Matterhorns, all within a short drive of Glasgow. I decided to hike up Ben Ledi, not far from Stirling; it would be my first proper mountain. The book gave grim warnings that it was a serious undertaking requiring proper equipment, so I duly hurried to the nearest hillwalking shop – called Nervous Sport or something like that – where I discovered that the manager was a String Band fanatic. I was guaranteed great service. I very rarely tell people about my muso days (some guys I've known for 20 years don't even know I play guitar), but, hey, if I think it will get me a little discount . . .

An hour later, I had all the gear: a rucksack, hillwalking boots, Gore-tex jacket, a compass and a book on how to use it. Oh, and another credit-card bill to explain away. How did I manage to spend *that* much? Oh, well. I decided that I would study the navigation book carefully. One day. As soon as I had time.

The next Saturday, I drove up to the small town of Callander at the foot of the hill. It was misty and cold, but the forecast was good. It was a pity there was no one to go with, but the furthest any of my friends walked was from the bar to the toilets. Joan wasn't interested in slogging up a hill; she simply smiled and gave me one of her looks, and I reckoned I should check the hill before taking my sons on it, assuming they'd want to go.

I followed the directions in the book and found the car park at the foot of Ben Ledi, just where Gilbert said it would be. It was almost empty. I had already packed my little rucksack and sat in the car rereading the instructions in the guidebook; it gave a step-by-step description of the way to the top. Deciding to learn by gradually getting experience on the hills was totally out of character for me – I usually have an initial eruption of enthusiasm, rush into something, make a complete bollocks of it and give up. Ben Ledi seemed a good place to start and, along with the fact it was only a short drive away, there were two other reasons I chose it.

According to the book, there is a small loch near the summit that centuries ago had been the scene of a mass drowning. Feeling very academic, I went along to the Mitchell Library in Glasgow to, eh, *research* this, and found some records from the eighteenth century. There it was. Apparently, a funeral party belonging to the Kessanach family had tried to walk across the loch when it was frozen. I wanted to see the loch because this baffled me – what was a funeral party doing that high up in the first place? It seems they were travelling to St Bride's Chapel on the other side of the hill. You would think the good citizens of the day would have known that ice breaks, especially if you take a bloody horse on it. Duh. How drunk would you need to be to walk that far off track? I reckoned I would check it out – Lochan nan Corp, the small lake of dead bodies. What a name! Sounded brilliant. The boys would think it was totally cool and peer into the water looking for skeletons. So would I.

The other reason was because the book said the name Ben Ledi was the shortened form of the Gaelic original Beinn le Dia, though I am completely unconvinced by all these translations the hillwalking writers knowingly churn out. This means, we are told, 'hill of god or light'. I hadn't been struck by any need for religion. I had read somewhere that ancient Druids used to gather at the top of Ben Ledi to have an annual get-together on 1 May, their New Year, light a huge bonfire and *par-tay* around it for three days. This sounded like an excellent idea. Any hill that had a history of feasting, drinking, drug-taking and scrums of sweaty bodies joined in lascivious sexual practices sounded exactly the mountain for me. And it was bound to be easy – how hard could it be if all those stoned, shagged-out revellers had managed to lurch to the summit every year?

Gilbert made finding the way very easy. If flat-pack instructions were written like his book, I wouldn't have a garage full of half-finished chests of drawers, and holes in the walls from throwing tools in exasperation. Feeling very excited, I started walking up a path through a forest, stopping every so often to study the guidebook. The route takes you beside a tumbling stream, then you turn left at a large boulder and walk up towards a main ridge where you turn right and carry on over a series of quite steep little humps and dips to the top. It was fine, you get in a rhythm; it's a lot easier than carrying heavy furniture up three flights of stairs.

I paused on the ridge for a gulp of water – this was thirsty work – wiped my sleeve across my forehead to catch the sweat running into my eyes and glanced down towards Loch Lubnaig. *Bloody hell, look at that!* Although the sun was shining out of a perfect blue sky, I was looking down on thick mist. It was colder below the mist than above, so everything was trapped under a dense, freezing blanket. Everyone in Callander would be pulling their coats around their necks and bitching about what a crappy day it was, yet up on the hill it was beautiful. I had never looked down on cloud like this, except from a plane. It was like standing on an island in the sky. In the distance, I could see the tops of dozens of shimmering mountains poking out of what looked like a vast white ocean into the brilliant sunshine.

I plodded on up the hill and, after an hour or so, reached the summit. Occasionally, I passed another walker and we would nod hello to each other as though we were conspirators enjoying a secret fetish. There was a cross near the top in memory of someone who had met his end on the mountain and, just beyond it, I put down my little rucksack, took out a cheese and tomato sandwich, a bar of Duncan's hazelnut (I think they may have gone out of business, but they used to make the best chocolate in the country) and a flask of coffee. Then I nearly dropped the lot – *I can see from one side of Scotland to the other!*

Ben Ledi doesn't get great reviews in hillwalking books, but it is in one of the best locations in Central Scotland; you can see so much from it. If anyone ever brings out a hillwalking version of Monopoly, Ben Ledi will surely be the equivalent of Trafalgar Square. Far away on my right, I could clearly see Arran rising out of the sea. I played with my new compass, waving it around like someone from the Starship Enterprise, as I tried to figure out if I was looking to the south, maybe south-west? Miles away, on my, eh, left, I could see Arthur's Seat in Edinburgh.

I hoped people would appear so I could share the amazing view with them. *I can see from one side of the country to the other. Coast to coast!* I sat for over an hour, bobbing my head from side to side, keeping my eyes open for any stray Druids; I could picture centuries of naked, fevered bodies leaping around the fire and . . . who am I kidding? I know nothing about the damn Druids. I had flicked through a few books and gathered that they believed in reincarnation and so, if I remember correctly, had contempt for written records, relying on memory to preserve their knowledge through the ages. The acid test of past lives. According to one book, the Northern Highlands was a Druidic stronghold for hundreds of years after the Roman conquest and over 1,000 years ago was a centre for students of the 'wicked arts of sorcery in its purest form', who travelled there from all over Europe . . . but enough of this.

I accept that I am easily irritated – too friggin' easily – but one of the things that annoys me about books on Scottish hillwalking are the smug, boring little references to recent history, things that happened in the last 200–300 years, especially when you think how ancient these mountains actually are. All these hairy-eared, tangly-bearded, real-ale-quaffing old farts warbling out romanticised trivia like, 'as I crested Sgurr Thuilm, I gazed on the summit, aye, the very spot where the Bonnie Prince passed a cold night with his men and . . .' Who cares?

I often went back to Ben Ledi and one December afternoon, a year or so later, I set off with a friend at about two o'clock to climb it. The mountain was covered in pristine snow; the nearest cloud was far out over the Atlantic. A full moon would rise soon after the sun disappeared behind the western hills. What could be nicer? As we climbed the fence leading to the large boulder, a pugnacious little weasel stopped us as he walked down to the car park. He stared at us, with a face like a nippy sweet.

'And where might *you* be going at this time of the day?'

My first reaction was to tell him we were looking for Callander High Street and must have taken a wrong turning, but I decided not to antagonise him and said we were heading for the top of the hill.

'But it will be dark in an hour!'

I looked at his huge, bulging rucksack, knitted hat, thick woollen pullover, heavy brown-leather boots and gaiters; the map hanging from his neck in a plastic folder; his wooden-handled ice axe; his moleskin trousers tucked into his thick socks at the knee and his bush-like beard with globules of tomato soup stuck in it.

'Well . . . yeah . . . I mean, yes, it will be. That's the general idea.'

'You mean you're going up the hill at *this* time of day?' he grimmaced, revealing teeth like a row of condemned buildings.

'Yeah, well . . . I can't get the sun to set any earlier.'

'Well, just don't expect *me* to rescue you!' He glared at us, snorted and strode off.

I wondered what he was ranting about – there's nothing new about hillwalking at night; Tom Weir wrote fascinating stories about the 1930s when loads of unemployed Glaswegians took to the hills. They enjoyed living rough in the mountains between signing-on days; it was far better than slouching around the street corners of Clydebank. They didn't have ultra-light, powerful halogen headtorches or high-tech clothes, they were tough bastards – used old *Daily Record*s as blankets. Eh, that's going a bit far.

More by accident than anything else, I had discovered that I loved going up to the top of a hill, watching the sun set, then coming back down in the dark by headtorch. You often don't even need one, especially when there's a full moon.

I'll always remember my first time sitting alone, high on a mountain, looking out towards the sea with the pastel colours gently blooming on the western horizon, then peacefully surrendering to the glittering stars that you can never see in a city. It wasn't joy I felt: it was a brief absence of pain.

A year after I started the business, my young brother had collapsed from a heart condition no one had suspected, and died alone in his rented flat. He was 26, a year younger than me. We had done everything together, all the childhood and teenage stuff: shared a flat, gone out drinking and clubbing. He was much calmer and quieter than me. He'd moved to Blackpool to be near his girlfriend and had put himself in debt more than once helping me when I had spent my rent on drink. Even though he'd left school at fifteen and needed two jobs to support himself, one of which was with a national charity where the pay was low, he had made sure I always had a guitar. I was heartbroken.

Then a close friend died suddenly, also from an undiagnosed heart problem. He was young, too. Stewart had been one of those real characters that people either loved or hated. He was a great yarn-spinner. At parties, you would find him surrounded as he bullshitted about how he had just returned from the North Pole where he had been 'wrasslin' huskies', or excitedly explaining his next great scheme for a business that would make us all rich. This annoyed some people – why couldn't he be *serious?* – but they'd missed the point: it was a lot more entertaining than listening to someone moaning about the government or drooling over the latest Ford Capri. He'd been the guy I talked to when my skin was crawling. Although not a drinker, he understood; any time, day or night.

I was in a daze. The sudden death of someone young is something you can only learn to live with, you never recover completely. Ever. These things happen, but you become horribly aware that everything can change in a second. I remember the exact moment I was told the body of my brother had been found; I remember how I was the instant before and how I have been ever since.

So when John Gilston, who had been the String Band

drummer, invited me out to Los Angeles to play in a band with him, I couldn't get on the plane fast enough. John had joined the ISB a few months after me and we had instantly become best friends, although our backgrounds couldn't have been more different. He'd attended an English public school and was a fantastic musician; he was a calm, thoughtful guy who brought out the best in everyone he met. People always felt good when he was around – as soon as he walked into a room, they'd smile. He had been living in LA for a few years and become a top session musician. In 1983, he played on five of the top-ten singles of the year, including 'Thriller' and 'Flashdance'. He'd really cracked it.

I loved to play bass with him; we both instinctively knew what the other would do, and we decided to work together as a rhythm section, picking up tours. We'd be happy to back anyone – from pop has-beens trying to wring the price of their next facelift out of their 20-year-old hits to God-rock bands playing to their massive swaying crowds. Anything at all, as long as there was a weekly cheque and they didn't look too closely at the room-service bills. With a bit of luck, something interesting would come along. People like Rod Stewart or Joe Cocker were always looking for solid bass and drums; backing musicians who would be happy to keep their mouths shut and play whatever the job required. John had got to know Ry Cooder quite well – they lived near each other and were doing some film work together – now that would be a tour I'd have done for nothing.

He had also teamed up with Nicky Hopkins, one of the world's top rock pianists at the time. John had formed a blues band with him and a few other hotshots; when I arrived in Santa Monica and played bass with them, I realised immediately how much I missed being in a pro band. This was where I belonged, doing what I loved. These guys were great players, far better than me, but I'd learned that playing simple stuff was much more effective than the 100-notes-a-second nonsense that so many flash LA bass players rattled out. I plugged an old Fender Jazz Bass into one of those big-ass Ampegs, those fat American amps that help anyone sound good, and concentrated on making the bass felt rather than heard; just sat in there with John's bass drum to give the guys with real talent something to build on.

I liked Nicky a lot. He was a fragile little guy who knew all about trouble with *the drink*. He'd worked with everybody: the Stones, Lennon, The Who; it would be easier to list the people he hadn't played with. If you sneezed in his house, you would hit a gold disc. The strange thing was that when he was swilling down brandy – and he was good at that (his size once helped him double the stake in a big-money sucker-bet against a hulking international rugby player in a Hong Kong drinking competition) – he had more offers of tours and sessions than he could handle. When he sobered up and started living a life that wasn't like an invading army, his telephone suddenly stopped ringing.

I didn't need to think about it – would you? I was sick of removals, had carried enough pee-stained mattresses to last a lifetime. I flew back to Glasgow and began getting ready to move to America with the family as soon as possible. The thought of the boys growing up hearing the surf and playing in warm Californian sunshine instead of dark, wet Glasgow streets was exciting. I couldn't wait to get there. John called me after an all-night recording session and we were like kids on Christmas Eve. We were set to go. He told me he was going to grab some sleep then drive the short distance to his favourite spot in Malibu for a little windsurfing.

John drowned that night.

7

DAYS

Small boys, big hills

DOING REMOVALS WASN'T EXACTLY MY DREAM OCCUPATION – NOT MANY KIDS long for the day they will earn a living carrying old furniture. It lacks the excitement of stepping onto a brilliantly lit stage in front of a sea of people in huge concert halls or at open-air festivals, playing guitar with the headline band – well, just a tad. But at least I felt I was in control of my life. And after I'd got back from John's funeral in Los Angeles, I just didn't feel like playing. I was numb.

I concentrated on the business and decided to give it my best shot, and spent any free time with my sons, taking them on walks in the hills – they loved making a game of it, dressing like commandos, carrying toy guns and all that stuff. We also couldn't resist having fun with some of the dreadfully serious characters we occasionally bumped into. One Sahara-like afternoon, we were coming down the access road from Loch Sloy when we noticed that there were dozens of slugs sunning themselves on the hot tarmac. I ran on ahead and put a black jelly-baby on the ground. We watched two heavily laden hillwalkers striding towards it, then my youngest son, Alan, who was about four, pounced on it shouting that he'd found a really fat one. He shoved it in his mouth as they stared in disbelief, thinking he'd just eaten a slug.

Hillwalking was becoming very popular. Muriel Gray's television series helped a great deal, and, as she pointed out, a beard was no longer mandatory. People were getting into it for all sorts of reasons: some simply enjoy the exercise of pounding up and down a mountain as fast as possible, like it's an open-air gym; others are only interested in ticking off another summit and couldn't care less about the view. What's wrong with that? I know two women who drop their kids off at school every morning then secretly hike up Dumgoyne Hill near Glasgow before tucking into a Perrier and no-carb salad lunch. Yum yum. They do it because it gives them energy, tones them and burns off enough calories to get into the little black dress that had so turned on their husbands in the first place. Lucky lads.

For some, sitting on mountaintops can be a mystical experience. It depends what your thing is. I usually sit and stare. *There's a feeling I get when I look to the west.* In autumn, I gaze in the direction of the warm south – all that Led Zep and Keats stuff. And, of course, I soon found that hillwalking is just the job if you're clamped into the treadmill of depression and there doesn't seem to be any way out.

It is very therapeutic to walk up Arthur's Seat or around the Pentlands, or any of those urban hills. An hour or so doing that, we are told, is more beneficial than Prozac. Apparently, German medics have proved this. They have some way of measuring how depressed you are – 'Ja, you are fucking crazy. Next!' There must be lots of guys wandering the Scottish hills at weekends who otherwise would almost certainly be locked up at night in the Happy Duck Rest Home for the Bewildered. OK, I admit it, I am one of them.

If you are addicted to alcohol, gambling, drugs or whatever, you live a complicated life; these are very demanding habits to maintain. The thing about Scottish hillwalking is that you have a simple objective. You stand at the bottom of a hill. Look up to the top. Point yourself in that direction. Walk there. Stop at the top. Sit down. Eat a cheese piece (if you are from Glasgow) or a ciabatta with mozzarella (if you are from Edinburgh). Drink some Irn Bru or sparkling mineral water. Admire the view. Feel good, or at least better than you did at the bottom. Turn round. Walk down. Go home and have a bath. No matter how lousy you felt at the bottom, you always feel better at the top. It is good for you. The Romans knew this. If you have a troubled mind, then it might be a good idea to walk it off a bit. If nothing else, you should be too tired out by the time you finish to do anything really stupid. Like reach for *the drink*.

Or drugs.

I had known plenty of musicians who took them, and hyped-up record company executives were notorious for snorting cocaine, or 'snozzola', as it was often called, but I was amazed at the number of guys running ordinary businesses, like little insurance offices and printing companies, who gulped down diazepam or similar crap, often with their nightly gin and tonic. At the time, bank interest rates were soaring and there were a lot of worried faces around.

Some scientist has found that hillwalking produces endorphins, the body's natural opiates or whatever; all I know is that it was the only thing that seemed to help me relax after a week of making sure there was enough work to keep the vans busy – the costs of running them were proving to be horrendous.

I'd done most of the hills near Glasgow and wanted to try something more remote. I still didn't know anyone else to go with, so I thought I'd better make an effort to learn how to read a map. Like other people who probably have an attention-deficit disorder, I am hopeless at sitting down and learning something methodically, but I didn't want to find myself clueless, cold, wet and starving in the middle of nowhere. When I was doing my daily house calls, trying to persuade people to hire us instead of Pickfords, I would have been lost without a street map, and I figured it was much the same thing.

I found that it is not very difficult to use a map and a compass, at least well enough that you don't end up hopelessly lost and lurching about for days like a fart in a trance. You are not attempting to locate the true North Pole, you're only trying to find your way around some bloody great hills sticking out of the ground without going the wrong way entirely or walking off a cliff. Most of the popular Scottish mountains have well-worn paths on them and, often, little piles of stones – cairns – which are a great help in mist, so, although many hills are a long way from civilisation, it is not like navigating across frozen Siberian wastes. A map and a compass can save a lot of hassle, like dying a slow, lonely and regretful death in the wilderness.

Ordnance Survey maps are works of genius; I am sure that in a couple of centuries they will be displayed on museum walls as a miracle of our age. Early edition maps will be sold at Christie's and become fashionable investments hanging beside old Fender Stratocasters and Gibson Les Pauls in New York City boardrooms. It will be inconceivable to a future generation why anyone would go to such trouble to draw in minute detail maps of the most remote and uninhabited parts of Scotland, using the very primitive means available to the OS prior to satellite imaging. I am in awe of the guys who spend their working lives in dusty little attic offices, sitting quietly at their drawing boards, puffing their pipes and pausing thoughtfully before meticulously curving that little red contour line a fraction east to catch more precisely the exact shape of some far-off little ridge in the deepest Highlands. Makes you shiver.

It would have been better to go on a course, like those run at Glenmore Lodge, but I just used a book and piddled around until I got the idea. It was exciting in a Davy Crockett kind of way. For once letting Joan know where I was heading and giving grim details of the time I should be back for my steak pie and hot bath (she's very accommodating), I wandered into the Campsie Fells, the nearest hills to Glasgow. They are like a miniature Cairngorms: flat on top and featureless, but with a few unmistakeable points that even I couldn't miss on the OS map. There is Dumgoyne, the volcanic lump like a rhino's horn jutting into the air that you can see from almost anywhere in Glasgow, along with Earls Seat and some large cairns. You can navigate from one to the other until you get the hang of it. I chose a sunny day and messed about taking bearings, following them with the compass until it dawned on me that, really, how difficult could it be?

The most important thing to be aware of, as I found out after finding myself temporarily misplaced a couple of times, is not where you are going, but where you are at any given moment. Strangely mirroring life itself, mystics might say. A compass is not much help if you are lost and can't see through mist to find anything you can use as a landmark. The new GPS gizmos are fantastic because it doesn't matter how cloudy or dark it is, you can pinpoint where you are on a map and navigate from there. As long as you remember the bloody batteries.

It seemed sensible, for once, to have some faint idea about what I was doing. Wandering up and down hills near Glasgow with my sons had been tremendous – the best days of my life – but they were getting older and naturally wanted to spend time with their friends. It had also kept me away from *the drink*, got me fit and helped me become confident to try higher, more remote mountains. The removal business was in a hell of a mess; instead of charging into building up the company, I should have taken one step at a time. I was now in trouble, big trouble. I needed to get out at weekends and do something that would take my mind off it, get some distance from it. Things were not working out as I had hoped.

8

WALK THIS WAY

The Munros

I RECKONED I'D REALLY BLOWN IT THIS TIME. COMPARED TO FINDING GIGS AND working with psychologically suspect musicians, I'd thought running a removal business would be easy. I rented a warehouse, picked up a load of contracts and had eight moving vans on the road. Oddly enough, I found it very helpful that I was used to always having about ten different things rushing through my mind at once; I was able to memorise at a glance all the jobs we had booked, then schedule the trucks in ways that ensured they covered the maximum amount of work; I could rearrange them all in minutes if necessary. I was enjoying seeing the company growing so fast. It was great fun.

Or so it seemed. It was all going beautifully when my biggest customer went bust and then, without warning, a couple of others decided to switch to other contractors. I was so naive. I hadn't realised the main reason the odds are stacked against new companies: the moment you start a business, you are elbowing your way into an already overcrowded marketplace. To get work, you have to steal it from the well-established companies that dominate it, but they haven't survived for years by being fools; they aren't going to just sit back and let you do that.

I kept on all the men, desperately trying to find other work. I had got the business into this shambles and I was determined to sort it. The weekly wages and running costs were crippling and, before I realised what was happening, I was in so much debt that if I had been a normal wage earner, it would have taken a century to clear. It wasn't a nice feeling looking at my sleeping kids and wondering if, next morning, the bank or the taxman would send in the sheriff officers and throw us on to the street. If that had happened, I'd have been declared bankrupt; it would have been years before I could have opened another bank account and without one it would have been impossible to save the business or even make a living. It would have been so easy to twist the cap off a bottle, but I knew other guys who had gone bust and the one thing they had in common was the thick smell of whisky on their breath by 8.30 in the morning.

Mickey moved to Wellington to marry a girl he'd met when he was driving the truck back from a removal job we'd done to London; she'd been hitching around the UK during that year-long trip to Europe so many people from New Zealand make. It was the smartest thing he ever did, but I missed him. Besides, he never drank on the job and had been a great help keeping the men sober when customers, trying to be nice, shoved cans of beer in their hands. *It's a hot day, lads, have a wee refreshment.* When removal men get drunk on the job, it's mayhem.

As I piled the bills in a heap on the old table I used as a desk, I felt sick. How could I have been so stupid?

Going off to the hills every weekend gave me a little breathing space. The great thing about the Highlands is that you can get there in less than an hour from Glasgow or Edinburgh and they are full of spectacular, soaring mountains. There are so many that way back in 1891 a climber called Sir Hugh Munro thought it would be a damn fine idea to make a list of all the

Scottish mountains reaching 3,000 ft and above. And it was. Most Scots, like me, had never heard of them until 1985 when a book called *The Munros* based on his list brought hillwalking to the high street. It was published by the Scottish Mountaineering Club, of which Sir Hugh had been president. It was well worth the 100-year wait.

The book calls on over a century's collective experience from skilled mountaineers who have found safe routes up and down almost 300 Scottish mountains, many in the most remote, unspoilt parts of the country. That in itself is a pretty nifty piece of work, but what made it especially useful is that the routes are presented in such painstakingly thought-out groupings that the mountains can be climbed in day trips by almost anyone. Thousands of people quickly realised that they could climb the Munros at weekends.

The book is beautifully illustrated with the routes simply drawn in red ink. A ten year old, even someone with the erratic mind of an ex-rock guitarist, could follow them easily. It is completely free of jargon: the reader is informed in a quiet, non-patronising way exactly what he needs to do to find his way to the top of mountains where only mountaineers had previously stood and gazed. By way of a bonus, it contains many of the most beautiful photographs ever taken in the Scottish Highlands. Every year at Christmas I send a copy to a friend or relation living overseas. Even if you never intend to climb a Munro, these pictures, possibly the only published photographs of many of the mountains, are well worth the price of the book.

Its publication was an admirable act of unselfishness, coming as it did from an apparently elitist clique of climbers who could not have been blamed if they had wanted to keep this hard-earned knowledge to themselves. The SMC is one of those old, highly exclusive private clubs that very easily attracts criticism, since hillwalking and climbing are supposed to be all about freedom. The SMC is *very* picky about accepting new members.

Most exclusive organisations have stringent membership requirements; golf clubs are well known for not accepting any old riff-raff, but they don't require prospective new members to be particularly good golfers, just as long as they don't excavate huge trenches with every whack of the ball. By comparison, membership of the SMC is by invitation only; all newcomers have to be shit-hot climbers at the very least and able to prove it. It also helps if you're male: as of January 2005, the club had only five female members out of a total of four hundred, although, of the countless climbers and hillwalkers I've met over the years, none has admitted to being in the club. Maybe they are a bit like the Masons; it's all a bit spooky. Of course, since membership is for life, many members are now OAPs – one wise-ass commented that you could always tell when the SMC were having their AGM by the clatter of Zimmer frames in the local hotel.

The SMC must have known the book would cause an explosion in the number of people taking to the hills and that not all of them would be as careful about removing their discarded banana skins as they themselves were. And it did. The book brought an awareness of the vast richness of the Scottish Highlands to thousands of people who, like me, did not know one mountain from another. The sport of Munro-bagging was born.

During the 100 years prior to its publication, fewer than 500 people had climbed all the Munros. In the 20 years that followed, at least another 2,500 did the lot, a huge number, bearing in mind that, of thousands of people from all over the UK who regularly climb Munros, only a small percentage finish the entire round. There are countless miles of driving involved; doing all the Munros is a colossal task and most people just do not have the free time, nor sufficiently sympathetic wives or husbands. It usually takes years. Many hillwalkers – probably the majority – have no plans to do them all; they can only manage one or two Sundays a month to go off with their pals up a hill. The rest of the time it's B&Q, Sainsbury's or playing with their children in the park, and they are perfectly happy with that. The SMC maintains a formal list of people who have climbed all the Munros; they call them *compleationists*. They are rather sniffy about this; anyone who *compleats* the Munros but does not submit their name to their clerk of the list is branded a 'dissident'.

I couldn't wait for weekends.

The first Munro I walked up was Ben Lomond, since it is the nearest one to Glasgow and there is a nice easy path all the way – which was fortunate because cloud completely obscured the last few hundred feet. When I reached the top, there was no one else around so I sat with my back against a concrete pillar placed by the Ordnance Survey. I wiped a Niagara of sweat from my face and lit a Dunhill. Hell, the occasional one couldn't hurt. I was well chuffed, but disappointed that there was nothing to see: only thick, cold, swirling mist, damp and clinging, sucking every last calorie of warmth from my bones. Then a gap appeared and I could see straight down to Loch Lomond, just for a moment, before the mist closed in again.

It was so exciting; it seemed an incredibly steep angle down to the loch. I felt as if I was on top of a huge Himalayan peak. Every so often, the cloud swirled open, giving me brief glimpses of the hills and valleys below. I kept jumping up and down, peering into the short partings in the mist, like looking down over a parapet from some kingdom in the sky. I was only getting teasing hints of the view from the top, but it was better than if the sky had been completely clear. It was unforgettable, like the first time you fly and look down through the night sky on thousands of pinpoints of light that are towns and villages glittering in the blackness, and how slowly they slip away underneath you. Scottish mountains are incredibly atmospheric in mist – and to think there were another 276 Munros just like this!

It was reckoned that there were only 31 mountains over 3,000 ft in Scotland until 1884 when a man called Robert Hall published a list of 236. This was quite an achievement because the OS did not get around to surveying many parts of the Highlands until well into the twentieth century. Though there is no record of Hall having actually climbed any of them, his list could have led to the hills being called 'Halls', which just doesn't sound right. And besides, the gentlemen of the Scottish Mountaineering Club could never have lived with the embarrassment of a non-climber having these mountains named after him. Sir Hugh's list, published seven years later, proved to be far more accurate, although he hadn't climbed them all either; it was a further ten years before anyone claimed to have completed them all, the Reverend A.E. Robertson.

Now, wherever lists and statistics are found, unfortunately so are little people with bony, pointy fingers, sharp nails, knobbly knuckles and far too much time on their hands. They write letters to *The Scotsman* correcting the editor on historical points of fact or the tartan worn by some obscure clan or other. They know all that stuff. They label all their videos and can zone in on any episode of *Weir's Way*, which they've recorded by carefully setting their timers to 2 a.m. They wear sandals with socks all year round and have great clumps of hair sprouting out of their ears. They grudge spending a penny on outdoor equipment, somehow feeling that shops should give it to them free. They submit long letters to the British Mountaineering Council's magazine; they're always harping on about something.

They have their framed compleationist certificates proudly displayed on their bathroom walls, but are not, they are adamant, *not* Munro-baggers. These bearded weirdies are fastidious in every possible life agenda from their local residents' association upwards; they drive everyone crazy. Hold on, am I going on too much? For some reason, hillwalking and climbing attract such people, and so even the good minister's word was questioned.

On the basis of a casual remark in his journal, a few people refused to accept that he had climbed Ben Wyvis, near Inverness, although it is one of the easiest Munros, just a gentle plod. You could push a pram up it. This was a man who routinely knocked off 70 Munros on short summer holidays, so

Wyvis would have been an easy stroll. The accusation that Reverend Robertson would lie about completing the Munros in that era, when a man's word was his bond, is distrustful to an unhealthy degree, but even today some people earnestly debate this over pints of home-brewed ale.

Another thing they do is fret and wring their hands over the accuracy of the list of Munros, send long letters to the OS questioning their measurements and generally niggle away for years to have hills included or deleted from the list. And so the book has been revised a couple of times, most recently in 1999, when seven new Munros were added to the list.

This had not come about, as some newspapers seemed to suggest, because hitherto unknown mountains had been magically discovered in the deepest Highlands. It was simply because the definition of an independent mountain was never set by Sir Hugh, nor has it been agreed upon since. Many Munros have false summits, as you notice with dismay when you're panting your way over them to the top. These are usually marginally lower than the highest point and have become known as 'Tops', although they are not regarded as the top of anything, if that's not too confusing. A few Tops that Sir Hugh listed as independent peaks have been relegated to supporting acts and others have been promoted to the big-time. The hairy-eared boys get quite fevered arguing about whether certain Tops merit inclusion in the list, or whether they are just outlying satellites of other Munros. Since they are the only people with the time to bother about such details, in the end, as is so often the case in life, they torment the hell out of everyone until they get their way.

This, and the fact that when revisions are made all sorts of new books, calendars and other products appear in the shops, suggests it is highly likely that the number of Munros will be changed yet again in the near future. It is a pity; many hillwalkers would rather respect Sir Hugh's original list and leave it at that; it's certainly close enough. You know you're not climbing every mountain in Scotland, just the ones he wrote down with his quill and ink, which has charm enough in itself. The thing is, when you have hauled your now-skinny bahookie up some Munros, stubbed out your very last cigarette and looked over your shoulder, especially in places such as Torridon, you realise that the list could be tinkered with endlessly; exactly where one mountain begins and another ends is often unclear.

There are also many spectacular mountains in Scotland just a little below 3,000 ft that you will probably never get around to climbing if you want to hold down a job and a marriage at the same time. Some mountains are Munros, some aren't, but no two are entirely the same. They are all beautiful; the Highlands are packed with hundreds of them.

The Munros should be given free to every school pupil; it is possibly the most important book ever published about Scotland and it has far wider-reaching benefits than simply providing reformed rock guitarists with something to do to keep them out of the pub at the weekend. For centuries, the Highlands suffered appalling acts of vandalism: the Clearances, when crofters had their homes burnt down and were deported because sheep generated more profit for landowners; the destruction of the beautiful native Scots pine forests; the mass industrial planting of alien Sitka spruce, the Big Mac of trees, enough to keep junk-furniture builders hammering for years; and inefficient hydroelectric dams (Scotland's mountains aren't high enough for them to work properly) forever submerging beautiful glens and replacing flowers and heather, birds, trees and rivers with grey concrete.

The book has created a huge army of cheerful environmentalists that takes to the hills every weekend. By making the public aware of these mountains and giving them a reason to walk up them, those who may have carried out further destruction have been halted in their Gucci shoes and wellington boots. Every inch of Scotland is owned by somebody, and some people own a great deal of it. If it wasn't for the ever-present attention of Munro-baggers, ignorant absentee landowners or self-serving lords of the manor might have quietly put up barbed-wire fences and restricted access to the glens and hills. Only a small number of people would have noticed: who would have cared if, like me, they didn't even realise what was there? Vast tracts of Scotland might have been fenced off and padlocked forever, reserved for bloated, port-drinking stalkers, churning up the ground with their Land-Rover tyres, armed to the teeth with double-barrelled shotguns ready to blast the living crap out of a few wee innocent grouse.

The Munros has contributed far more to the preservation of the Highlands than any twee tales about Bonnie Prince Charlie – these damn kings believed they were God's direct descendants and the rest of us just cattle to be ruled – or songs about wee bonnie boats sailing over the sea to Skye. It has quietly and democratically offered Scotland to its people and inspired them to use and love it. That is one hell of an achievement for any book.

9

WILD WORLD

White snow in dark places

THE BUSINESS WAS STUMBLING ALONG. I WAS BALANCING OVERDRAFT AGAINST debt, collecting money as fast as possible and praying none of the trucks broke down. No sooner had I dealt with one crisis than another would crash through the door. It was driving me crazy. You might think that such a precarious existence would provide enough excitement, but I seem to be one of those people who just cannot live without some kind of lunacy going on. And as usual, it didn't take me long to find some.

I'd heard that in settled, crisp cold weather, when covered in snow and under a clear blue sky, the Highlands are stunning. There might be places in the world as beautiful, but it would take a lot more than an hour or so to drive to them; you can get the atmosphere of the Karakoram or the Himalaya without the dysentery, which suits me fine. In winter, Scottish mountains can be extremely dangerous and are often used as a training ground by people about to climb K2 or Everest. At the risk of stating the blindingly obvious, you have to be careful: snow-clad beauty comes at a price.

The first time I climbed a mountain in winter, I nearly came down a lot faster than I went up. I was with a guy I met through the business, a sales rep, and he had assured me he knew everything there was to know about mountaineering. We were standing on the top of Ben More, high above Crianlarich, with only an hour or so of daylight left, the temperature was dropping fast and the snow was starting to freeze. We had no ice axes or crampons; it was time to go down.

My pal was one of those cheery characters who sail along on the surface of life, hopelessly optimistic about everything; the sort of guy that used-car dealers love. He could have been in a burning house and all he would have noticed was that his arse was lovely and warm – he simply couldn't imagine that anything bad might happen. He chirped on about how easy it would be to continue along the ridge to the top of Stob Binnein, another Munro nearby, and I felt I was being a bad-tempered fart when I suggested that he was crazy to even think about it.

It is always easier to go up than down, especially over hard-packed snow and, as I plodded on, muttering to myself, I didn't realise how dangerous the mountain was becoming. By the time we'd reached the top, watched the sun disappear, almost broken a couple of teeth on a frozen Mars bar, gulped down some water, then started coming back down, the side of the mountain had frozen solid and the north-facing slope, the only way off, was now a dark, treacherous ice field. We picked our way down – it seemed to take hours, tentatively balancing on the sharp points of little rocks pointing up through the horribly steep frozen ground. One slip and we would have hurtled down, impossible to stop, the rocks and boulders ripping the cracks of our arses to our ears. I shouted and swore at him all the way to the road; farmers for miles must have heard us yelling at each other. I haven't seen him since.

As soon as I could get to Nervous Sport, I bought a pair of crampons and an ice axe. It meant another credit-card bill to explain away, but it was so beautiful in the snow-covered mountains that I couldn't wait to get on them again. I wanted to avoid the New Year's Day drinking sessions so drove to another mountain near Crianlarich called An Caisteal. Having crampons strapped to your boots is great: you just scrunch across ice or frozen snow and up you go – they grip like claws. What hadn't occurred to me was that you have to be sensible enough to realise that they can get you into places you shouldn't be in unless you are a climber, or at least know what you are doing. I wasn't and I didn't.

After a few hours' steep but easy walking, I stood at the top of the mountain looking down a short ridge invitingly leading to another Munro, Beinn a' Chroin.

I had forgotten to bring the route instructions from *The Munros*, but it looked easy enough; all I had to do was cut diagonally upwards a little way across an easy-angled snow slope. Above that, I could see another short, slightly steeper section that quickly eased off, becoming a gentle walk to the top. No problem, I could do that! Kicking steps up the hard-packed snow, I soon reached a ledge below the steeper section and whacked my ice axe into the slope above it. *Boing!* The axe bounced out with a metallic ring. *What the . . .?* Suddenly, I realised it wasn't snow, it was a slab of rock covered by marble-hard ice. *Oh, no.* I tried again. *Boing!* I gulped. *What the hell now?* I looked down. *Oh, fuck.* The snow ledge I was standing on was disintegrating under my feet.

I quickly learned two things. The first was that if you climb diagonally upwards to a ledge and it collapses, you will fall, but not back across the same easy angle you came up. I glanced at my feet and realised that I was about to plummet straight off a very high cliff. The second thing I learned was that when you are scared shitless, your heart actually does pound so hard you can hear it. I realised that if I didn't move immediately, I would be dead in a crumpled heap at the foot of the cliff. Saying this takes a lot longer than it took for me to recognise what a bloody stupid thing I had done – *what the hell am I playing at?* – and desperately launch myself back across to safe ground. It wasn't so much a blind panic, more an adrenalin-driven terror.

After that, I realised it would be safer hillwalking in winter if I was with other people. I had done a couple of hills with women and they had been good company; they avoided stupid risks and talked about books and films and stuff. Men usually farted and grunted their way up as quickly as possible, gulped down a stale cheese sandwich, then charged back down for a pint in the nearest pub, which was the *last* thing I needed. And I was utterly bored hearing about their latest sexual conquests or how virile they'd been last night, as if sustaining an erection for more than three minutes was an act of heroism.

I often met interesting people on the hills. One of the women I walked with was a university lecturer who I'd bumped into on a Munro near Killin. She had been married to an Australian she'd met in a backpackers' hostel when she was a post-grad trekking around Tibet or Thailand or some place. One of those dumb things you do. They'd known each other only weeks before the wedding; it had seemed a good idea at the time. She'd escaped his sheep farm eight years previously, tired of his rough hands, his huge thundering belches, Fosters lager with everything and, damn it, a NASA countdown had more tenderness. His foreplay had been unvarying, always starting with the hiss of the sixth can opening and some remark about hauling her *hiney over here, honey.*

She'd landed a good job in Edinburgh and had worked hard to get to her current post. Now 30-something, as they say in the personal columns, she knew what was missing – a good man. But it was difficult. Like many of her friends, she almost placed an ad in *The List*, a magazine in which lonely hearts throughout Central Scotland eagerly search for dream dates, but these pleading calls for companionship made her squirm. They were all looking for a 'Soulmate for ltr, n/s with gsh who likes sunsets, beach walks and cosy nights in/out.' Hell, she knew exactly what she would say, but doubted they'd print it:

Well-hung guy wanted, any old bloke will do, but must
NOT:

   a) be married

   b) be gay

   c) live with his mother

   d) believe that Elvis is still alive

   e) spend his spare time learning to speak Klingon

All of which pretty much applied to just about every man
she'd dated since she'd returned to Scotland. Short of
abducting a schoolboy and moulding him, she didn't know
what she would do. The needs of the flesh are strong,
however, and she had been in an on–off relationship with a
professional footballer for almost two years. He was married,
but, being highly competitive, fit and good-looking, he liked
plenty of variety. What really turned him on was the way he
could control women through sex – he knew how subservient
he made her feel and he thrived on it.

She despised herself for the way she would always let him
into her snug, book-lined flat, her Georgian conversion in the
city's New Town, whenever he rang the bell. She knew the
only reason he came round and she hated the weak way she
always gave in, but his body was simply perfect . . . she just
couldn't say no. *This would be the last time.* She was highly
intelligent, rational in every other aspect of her life, but over
him she was powerless. All her friends were utterly bored
hearing about it; every latte she shared with them ended in
sobbing, as she vowed she would call him tomorrow,
definitely, this time she would, and tell the bastard to bugger
off for ever. She'd quit a pack-a-day without the slightest
relapse, but him . . .

Much of our time hillwalking together was spent bitching
about our problems: the delights of running a 20-employee,
hopelessly debt-ridden company or the torment of *the
footballer*, as she called him. *The fucking footballer thought I
was with someone else and parked outside half the night*

watching my flat. Who the hell does he think he is? That was the other thing about him, the worst thing: he didn't allow her to be with any other man. Or else.

When she was in a good mood, which was most of the time, she was brilliant company, always had a funny story to tell or a great book to talk about. One summer's day, we'd walked through beautiful Glen Nevis, inched across a superb, steel-cabled bridge swaying above the river and plodded up to the Ring of Steall, a circular group of mountains linked by the steep, mind-concentrating Devil's Ridge. The weather was perfect; hours of warm July sunshine lay ahead of us. As we walked round the narrow ridge, she quoted a line from Shakespeare, then another, and another. Hearing those gently lilting phrases in such beautiful scenery was simply magical. I won't twitter on about the sounds of streams and soaring mountain views and all that stuff – you can imagine.

I hate to be critical . . . bollocks, no, I don't . . . but when I was at school, I hated the way my English teachers made such a mess of passing on any enthusiasm for the great writers. I mean, did Shakespeare have a way with words, or what? They handed us a play and gruffly told us to read it aloud in the class. It was excruciating. That sing-song drone – if *mu-sic* be the *food* of love – put us off for life. You would think that in Glasgow, where violent, illegal money lending was rife, we would have enjoyed *The Merchant of Venice* if it had been presented in the right way. I suspect things aren't any different today: kids love Eminem and watch *Friends* for hours, but tell you they hate poetry and theatre.

It was fascinating; as we hiked up and down our weekly Munros, she would always have some quote or other, or she would talk about the many trips she had made to India, though I'll never understand why she smiled wistfully as she fondly recalled sleeping on a rat-infested platform in some backwater village while she queued for two days to buy a train ticket to some other equally remote outpost.

One winter, we decided to do a hill called Creise, near

Glencoe Ski Centre. We reckoned we could climb it, then catch a free ride down on the chairlift. The snow lay like a thick carpet right down to the road – great skiing conditions, although the forecast was for high winds and blizzards, but they weren't due until that night. Plenty of time, we thought, as we climbed the far side of the mountain, away from the ski runs. As we neared the top, a light flurry of snow began falling, the wind picked up and before we knew it we were in a white-out. The storm had arrived early and it was ferocious. A climber died on the Cairngorms when the cold gripped her with such an intensity that it sucked the life from her body.

Fortunately for us, we were on a more sheltered mountain, less exposed to the arctic winds, but by the time we managed to push through the blizzard in the direction of the ski lifts, the hill was deserted and it was almost completely dark. In falling snow, the light from your headtorch bounces back at you, like car headlights on thick fog, so it is very easy to become lost. We managed to find our way to a locked ski hut where we stopped and sheltered as best we could, unable to see anything but snow howling around us.

There was a slight lull and we managed to get our map out without the wind ripping it from our hands and checked where we were. We were still high on the mountain and leaned back against the wall of the shed, reluctant to risk going any further. Down below, to the left of the main ski lift, a deep stream tumbles and surges hundreds of feet down a gully and if we stumbled over the edge, it would be thank you and goodnight – her relationship hassles and my work problems would be solved, permanently. This was no place to be blundering around in a storm. If we had been on any other mountain, we might have been terrified and huddled together like shivering hamsters, but although we were thousands of feet up, we knew that we were safe beside the hut. If we had to, we could break in and spend the night there.

Then, as quickly as it had arrived, the wind dropped, the

sky cleared and suddenly we could see hundreds of stars. The storm had passed through, leaving a thick covering of fresh snow. We stood quietly in the darkness, alone on the vast mountain, breathing softly in the silence, saying nothing.

We had just started walking when 'the Lecturer' felt her feet shoot out from under her and she rocketed down the steep snow slope into a dip in the hill, giggling the whole way. The snow was firm, but not icy. She clambered back up with her ice axe, brushed the powder off and we continued down. I was happily walking, looking at the dark, silver-studded sky when suddenly I was on my back sliding head-first downhill. It happened so fast I didn't realise I had fallen on one of the ski runs, which *was* firm and icy. I managed to turn over enough to slam the point of my axe into the slope and throw my weight on it. I ground to a halt. We couldn't stop laughing.

At last, we reached the pylons that carry the chairlifts uphill from the car park. We knew that if we stayed to the right of these, we would avoid the icy river crashing down the hill. Falling into a steep stream is fatal – as the water forces its way under hard-packed snow and ice, you'd be pulled below and trapped underneath, perhaps a long way downhill from where you fell in. A horrible way to die.

We kicked our heels deep into the snow as we plodded down in the direction of the car park far below. We could see the last couple of 4x4s leaving and watched their tiny little headlights as they picked their way onto the main road, then were swallowed up in the darkness. Then the moon slid out, lighting the whole glen in a soft, yellowish glow like muted stage spotlights. We stopped; it was too beautiful to speak.

We stared around the white, snow-covered mountains. They seemed to almost hover above the glen, quietly glowing and pulsing in the moonlight. Suddenly, we felt that we had entered their time, much greater and deeper than our own, as though we were held in a pause. We realised that whatever problems we had in the city, these hills would always be there, a touchstone to reality.

'There's something about this place . . .' she said.

'I know,' I replied, very quietly, sharing the same thought.

For a moment, in that vast silent land, you could almost hear the mountains breathe.

10

ALL RIGHT NOW

Aonach Eagach

IF YOU READ THE OUTDOOR MAGS, IT'S NOT ENOUGH TO STROLL UP A HILL – THEY are full of battle cries about tackling mountains, personal challenges, pushing yourself to the max and all that happy horseshit. They provide interesting reading – I have piles of them in the bathroom – but for most of us the biggest challenge, and certainly the hardest, is staying one mortgage payment ahead and bringing up kids you hope don't go over to the 'Dark Side', or at least not permanently.

Is it not enough to be crawling along in the snarling commute every morning, just managing to dodge a psychotic breakdown and keeping your bitching boss off your case? I suppose some people can spend their lives purposefully striding ahead of their laden Sherpas or dodging crevasses and polar bears as they stagger single-handedly to the North Pole, but supporting a family is the North Face of the Eiger that confronts most of us on a daily basis; anything else is just fun. Or should be.

If you can face the responsibility of bringing up children and holding down a job in the hire-and-fire conditions we face these days and not end up twitching in a permanently dark room gulping down G&Ps (gin and Prozac), then you really have achieved something. Especially, dare I say it, if you happen to be in the removal business. Customers are so wound up by the time moving day rolls around, they invariably take it out on the removal company. It is a time-sensitive business: you have to have the punctuality of the speaking clock, regardless of blizzards, icy roads, illness or, crucially, whether Rangers beat Celtic the day before, in which case half your staff will be unconscious or just AWOL. Instead of starting their working week bright-eyed in the van, they will be waking up with a brain-shattering headache and probably a well-kicked arse in a 6x9-ft cell, waiting for the judge to deal with their drunk-and-disorderly charge . . . as the Ibrox support happily sings, 'no one likes us and we don't care'.

There's nothing you can do about it; they just breeze in a few days later with a self-certified sick note. (I always played the odds by making sure that the other 50 per cent of my men were Celtic supporters. That way, no matter who won, at least half the workforce would turn up. If you were a 'Jags' supporter – or Partick Thistle Nil, to give them their full name – you were guaranteed a job.)

The removal vans have to get to their jobs bang on time; they have to inch down narrow streets and squeeze by cars parked so far out from the kerb you would have trouble getting a bike past them – this is particularly bad near train and Underground stations where commuters leave their cars strewn all over the place in their rush to catch the 8.15 into town. In some Glasgow suburbs, residents deliberately leave as little room as possible for other vehicles to pass: they don't want lorries using their leafy avenues and lowering the tone of the neighbourhood. Four removal men can bounce most cars out of the way – Mickey and I once lifted a Mini onto the pavement – but it's a hassle and wastes time. And there's always the chance the car belongs to some psycho ex-boxer.

Setting all that to the side, moving house isn't life-and-death, and all the statistics about it being one of the most stressful things you can do are just part of a conspiracy to line up more customers for trendy aromatherapists and life-coaches. You can make anything stressful, even going to buy a pizza – it depends entirely on your point of view. I loved touring with the band, seeing all those foreign countries, yet some musicians spent their time wringing their hands in luxury hotel rooms writing pathetic songs about how tough it is to be on the road. Nonsense – it's long hours, but far easier than the average 9-to-5 shift. You get a big cheer from the audience at the end of your day's work, a limo to the nearest Hilton and can get laid in nice clean sheets every night if you feel like it. What other job gives you that? Just depends on your point of view. Moving house is not stressful. It's all in the mind.

Much like the Aonach Eagach Ridge.

If you are ticking off Munros, it is only a matter of time before you have to get your hands out of your pockets and do a bit of climbing. They are mountains, after all. The first climby sort of ones most hillwalkers do are on the Aonach Eagach Ridge, the narrowest ridge on the British mainland, the one I'd looked up at all those years ago when we'd driven through Glen Coe: long, dark and very steep, like the battered walls of a massive Gothic fortress.

This is where one of the oddities in climbing – and there are many, as I was to discover – enters the picture. From a point of view of difficulty, climbers do not regard Aonach Eagach as a climb at all. It is merely a *scramble*. Oh, well, that's all right then. They mean that, in dry conditions, it has no *technical* difficulty: anyone not dependent on a Zimmer frame can scramble across it; it is no more difficult than the beachside rocks we used to play on as kids. Of course, if you fall at sunny Ayr, you will land a few feet below on a nice sandy beach; if you fall from the Aggie Ridge, it could be 3,000 ft before what's left of you splats in front of some startled driver on the road below. You have to be confident on your feet and not worry about the amount of air beneath them. So if you start quivering when you are up a ladder changing a light bulb, it might be best to think again.

Scrambling is more dangerous than rock climbing; climbers know this, but rarely crack a light about it. Rock climbing is much more difficult, and requires knowledge of technique and equipment and all that palaver, but if you fall, you are tied to a rope, so the chance of being hurt is minimised. If you are scrambling, there is nothing to stop you bouncing all the way down to the deck. Elvis has left the building.

The biggest dangers in scrambling are slipping, a hold breaking off or someone knocking a chunk of rock down on your noggin. If you can relax (which is essential, because if you are stiff with tension, you will not be able to climb at all), scrambling is an exhilarating experience. It is far scarier to stand on the narrow platforms of the London Underground when the five o'clock crowd is jostling for space. There is a fabulous feeling of freedom when you clamber up an airy ridge of easy-angled solid rock using comfortingly large handholds. And there are no glassy-eyed psychos waiting to elbow you in front of a train.

Since I knew nothing about this scrambling malarkey, I thought it wise to do Aonach Eagach with a guiding company, and chose one from Stirling. I reckoned it was best not to take the thing lightly – people had been seriously hurt or killed falling off it. I drove up to Glen Coe tingling with apprehension and met their minibus full of excited clients in the large car park across from the start of the steep path up to the ridge.

They had a couple of those freshly scrubbed outdoor instructors, who proved to be very good. They strapped harnesses around our waists, told us they had ropes, just in case, and off we set. One of them pointed out that climbing comes naturally; even people who are clumsy on the ground can swarm up the steepest sections of the ridge without any problems. He told us always to stay balanced, not to overstretch, and to take little steps rather than attempt to make long lunges, something I realised would have been handy if I'd thought of it before I'd got into so much debt buying trucks. It was a pleasant June day, the rock was clean and dry, and we all found clambering along the ridge easy; there were plenty of big rocky holds for our hands and feet on the steep bits; great fun, although in rain or during winter it would be a completely different proposition.

Glencoe Mountain Rescue Team is regularly called out to the ridge when people become stuck after trying to escape from it. One thing I noticed, duh, is that you get tired when you are wandering around the hills. When that happens, your ability to think clearly drops significantly and, because of this, you do not realise it. I was soon aware that it is a very good idea to have little rules, or mantras, that echo in your brain like an irritating Boney M song. These can easily save your hide.

One of them is 'there are no shortcuts off'. I proved this more than once after sitting knackered on a hill and taking what looked like an easy, shorter route down, only to find myself ploughing knee-deep through peat bogs, crawling on my face under dense Sitka trees and finally wading through streams to emerge at the roadside hours later than anyone else, causing great hilarity because I looked like someone who had just been pulled from an earthquake.

I use loads of them: check the map; trust the compass; watch the weather; always know where you are; stop and think; shut the fuck up, and so on. Actually, I should use the last one on myself a lot more. The point is, if these things are embedded, they come to you whenever you need them. I began to do this in the business, too. Always have a back-up plan. Never sack a drunk, wait until he has a hangover. Don't mess with the taxman. Don't argue with anyone. Imagine the customer is your mother. Don't promise what you can't deliver. Most customers are great, don't let the few who aren't get to you. Trust yourself.

The next time I did Aonach Eagach, I was with a guy with

whom I had briefly played in a band – briefly because it was one of those shitty cabaret outfits. *Moon river, wider than a mile.* I sat in with them a couple of times; I think they were called Cash Money and The Fiddles. The taxman won't have a note of them, but we'll gloss over that. We were doing some Christmas dance or other at a very posh hotel complex at Loch Lomond, and Bono and The Edge were there, having a quiet drink, sitting near the little stage beside the small, circular dance floor all these places seem to have. The minute we began playing, a startled look came into their eyes and they edged away pretty bloody fast. I don't think we influenced U2's next billion-selling album.

It was about lunchtime on an unusually hot, midweek summer's day when my pal's car finally appeared. He leapt out with the unmistakable flushed and dehydrated look of a man who has, as he had, rattled through a bottle of wine and several vodkas the night before. I looked at his bloodshot eyes and pale face.

'Are you sure you're up for this?'

'Yeah, no problem. I'll be fine when I get going.'

'You look pretty rough.' It had been a long time since I'd had a drink, but I could remember exactly how he was feeling.

'Mouth's as dry as a rodent's rectum. Fuck it, I'll be fine. Let's do it.'

His hands were twitching as he tossed down an entire litre-bottle of water in a gulp; I swear you could almost hear his parched skin crackle. We started the steep plod up to the start of the narrow ridge, the sun microwaving us from a cloudless sky. I have always loved the heat of the sun – I mean, what is it with these people in Glasgow who, as soon as a rare hot summer's day comes along, start whinging as though they were stranded in the Sahara? *It's awfy close, isn't it, hen? I'm roastin'.*

He was struggling. He had gurgled down another litre-bottle and refilled it with water tumbling down the hill. I have always been wary about drinking from streams since the day I noticed the carcasses of three sheep rotting in one. My friend was far too dehydrated to bother. He would have drunk anything. He was sweating pure alcohol; you could smell it seeping from every pore. His face was like a collapsed building. He took a bite from a stale-looking sandwich and I could see his stomach lurch. He looked dreadful.

'Are you sure, I mean, really sure, you want to do this today?' I looked at him sympathetically.

He grinned – well, sort of – and seemed to have trouble swallowing. 'Yeah, I'll be fine in a minute. Feel much better already. Been wanting to do this for years. Eh, give us a drink of your water, will you?'

'It's just that once you go on the ridge, there is no way off it. You either have to come back to the start or continue all the way to the end.'

'I'll be fine. See, I'm brand new.'

So, off we set.

The sun beat down like an exploding supernova. We hadn't even reached halfway before he had drunk every drop of water we had. And still it got hotter. When I stopped to pee, it was a dark yellow trickle; I could have struck a match on my tongue, but it felt great to be so high above the glens on either side of the ridge. We could see all the way past Ballachulish to the sea – when the sun shines on Scotland, there's nowhere as beautiful.

We were managing to keep up a fair speed, despite the heat. The lure of cold, sparkling lager at the pub in Glencoe pulled my mate forward, his bloodshot eyes staring straight ahead. We kept looking, but couldn't find a drop of water anywhere and as we reached the end of the ridge, he began staggering like someone lost in the desert. My mouth felt as though there was an old tennis ball wedged inside it, but he was so dehydrated he must have been sucking up brain matter. Then he yelled like a man winning a Vegas jackpot and threw himself on the ground, pushing his face into a tiny trickle of brown water bubbling out of a hole.

He grovelled and slobbered and sucked and lapped at it, spitting out lumps of muck and clusters of insects. He turned his baked face up to me, mud and dirt hanging from his mouth, 'Aw, brilliant, just brilliant.'

And it was.

11

VERTIGO

The Bookie

CHANCE MEETINGS FASCINATE ME; THEY ARE ONE OF THE THINGS THAT MAKE life exciting. Who knows who you might meet today? Many years ago, Keith Richards bumped into Mick Jagger in a train station and noticed he was carrying Muddy Waters records. They got talking and eventually took all those obscure Chuck Berry, Muddy Waters and Howling Wolf songs and anglicised them, changing music for ever. Pseudo-intellectuals whinged that the Stones, Yardbirds and Zep ripped off the old bluesmen, but it is romanticised drivel. British and American kids still buy Muddy Waters and Willie Dixon records 50 years after some of them were recorded; that would never have happened if it hadn't been for the Stones.

Occasionally, you miss meeting someone interesting because you are too busy thinking about other things. One of the String Band's road crew kept telling us that his girlfriend was a terrific songwriter but somehow no one got round to listening to her until one night she appeared on Top of the Pops. It was Kate Bush.

Sometimes a seemingly minor, last-minute decision, like going to the pub the night you met your future ex-wife, has such consequences that you feel the gods should have told you the next choice you made was going to change your life completely – a spotlight shining down would be helpful. And so, one cold night I met a climber called Alex Mayes in the Kelvin Hall sports centre in Glasgow as we jogged round the indoor running track. He was training for a trip to the Alps; I was just trying to keep warm.

I recognised him because he lived just across the road from my house, and, like me, usually didn't bother to socialise with the people who lived nearby – *wouldn't it be nice if I got on with me neighbours?* He mentioned that he owned a couple of hillwalking shops called Summits. We got talking about Munros we'd done and I was stupid enough to say I'd found Aonach Eagach easy, so he decided to up the stakes.

'Why not try a bit of rock climbing?'

He is charismatic, with a friendly, relaxing grin that I would learn to be wary of, especially if whatever he was urging me to do included something like, 'Come on, it's a dawdle.' I was too gullible to know better and a month or so later was halfway up Buachaille Etive Mor at the side of a dark, steep gully, staring up a long, vertical crack in a huge, black rock face called Rannoch Wall, which was looming menacingly over us.

Jesus Christ, he wants me to climb this?

The Bookle, as it is called, is probably Scotland's most photographed mountain; the Brad Pitt of the Highlands. It appears on calendars in every tourist shop because you can stand well back from it on Rannoch Moor and, as it thrusts its pelvis over a tumbling stream, comfortably frame its triangular shape, which is exactly the sort of pyramidal form that publishers like mountains to take. If you look at any of these pictures, below the summit and slightly to the left of the centre you can see Rannoch Wall, slinking back like a mugger in a doorway. It doesn't look half as big or threatening as it does close up, by which time it's too late. When I called my pal in

Nervous Sport and asked him if this would be a good place for my first climb, he said he thought Alex must be insane. That sounded about right. I had decided to go for it anyway.

One of the first things Alex patiently taught me about rock climbing is that you don't just walk to a cliff and start clambering up it. Rock climbing is far from the carefree, anarchic sport I had imagined it to be; the province of swashbuckling modern-day adventurers sailing, as it were, in boundless freedom on an ocean of uncharted rock. It is very dangerous, so climbers have developed rules to protect the unwary, like me, and Alex carefully explained some of them.

The first thing I learned is that climbing is methodical; it follows exact and specific *routes* up rock faces and all routes have names. Not John or David or anything like that, but usually something clever and dramatic, often with mystical or biblical overtones such as Satan's Slit, Crack of Doom or Polyphemus Gully. The name is chosen by the first person who climbs the route; this is then sacrosanct and never changed, even after a few bright sparks in the '60s christened some new, desperately hard routes Strapadicktaemi, Minge, Phellatio and Cunnulinctus, which annoyed many older members of the climbing establishment. I mean, what kind of spelling is that?

As I peered doubtfully up the crack, Alex buckled an old, frayed harness around my waist and tied a suspiciously thin green and orange rope to it. He then cheerfully informed me that we were at the foot of a well-known route called Agag's Groove and this is what we were going to climb or 'do', to use his exact expression. Climbers talk about 'doing routes' when they climb things. This sounded great – I am always delighted to learn new expressions that only insiders use. When I was playing in bands we never used 'gig', we always just said we 'had a job on' or were 'working' that night, especially after DJs and even comedians – I mean, spare me – hijacked the word.

Anyway, the angle of the rock was steep, but from where we were standing, it didn't look too difficult, mainly because the sheer size of the rock face above didn't show itself at that point.

What the hell, I thought, how hard can it be? He said the climb was graded as being very difficult, which, in climbing terminology, meant that it was easy.

I took a very deep breath. *OK, we've come this far. Let's do this.*

Alex handed me a lump of metal with two circular rings in the shape of the number eight. This, he told me, was a belay device. He fed the rope through it, then clipped it to my harness. It was designed to allow me, extremely optimistically on his part I felt, to arrest his headlong plummet to the ground if he fell. In trusting me this way, he totally failed to appreciate how long it takes me to grasp the workings of even the most basic mechanical objects. This lack of any understanding of the laws of physics had not helped me in operating a fleet of high-maintenance removal trucks. It was perfectly obvious to grinning garage owners that I knew less than the average schoolgirl about engines and they could charge me anything they wanted. If they'd told me that the headlights needed a replacement candle or that the prop shaft required a new heavy-duty rubber band, I would have believed them. I just grimly nodded in a manner that I hoped looked knowledgeable and wrote out the cheque.

I only mention this because it is amazing how many people back off from starting a business just because they know nothing about it. *When you've got nothing, you've got nothing to lose.* You just do the best you can, learn as you go and don't let utter ignorance hold you back. So, if Alex thought that he would be safe in my hands if he fell, he was dreaming. It never occurred to me that I would join him at the bottom in a mess like a mixture of potato salad and raspberry pavlova since we were tied into opposite ends of the same rope.

Alex handed me an old pair of pink-coloured climbing shoes – yes, pink; climbers are very fashion conscious – and I crushed my toes into them. They were like ballet shoes, but tighter than clamps and I could feel every little stone beneath my feet. If I had been standing on an ant, I could have told you whether it was male or female. He thrust his hands deep into a chalk bag tied round his waist, wiggled them about a bit, blew on his fingers, looked up above, grinned contentedly, then gracefully snaked up the crack until he was out of sight. He made it look easy. I fed out the rope to him – well, sort of – until eventually it pulled tight.

'OK, up you come.'

My turn. *Here goes then. Stay calm. Enjoy it.*

I followed the line that he had taken and suddenly I was climbing. Years of carrying heavy amps and furniture had made me strong and this suited me fine. Climbing felt good. The holds were not as big as on Aonach Eagach, but there were plenty of them and, because I was climbing in a crack, I didn't feel any real sense of height – I just concentrated on looking up towards the next hold. If I did look down, the angle was such that I could see rock beneath my knees so I didn't feel at all nervous. Up I climbed, higher and higher.

Hey, this is fun!

I reached Alex on a ledge where we could both stand comfortably side by side, and he clipped me to some . . . well . . . some clanky bits of metal he'd jammed into cracks in the rock; it all looked very precarious. He was totally relaxed; this was home ground for him. He told me that his 'gear' was 'bomber' and wouldn't 'rip', which I hoped meant that whatever he'd attached me to was safe. He assured me you could 'hang an elephant off it'. Excellent, more new expressions. He pointed behind me and I looked over my shoulder at the vast plateau of Rannoch Moor, stretching away to the east. *This is it, the big-time. I'm actually rock climbing!*

Alex checked I still had the belay device connected to the rope and he was away again, climbing higher up the rock. The rope went tight again, so I clambered up and joined him on another ledge, rested for a moment, then he climbed on. He shouted to me to follow him and I stepped out, following the rope. Suddenly, the rock face steepened and I realised with a sickening jolt that I was hundreds of feet off the ground. I had never known anything like it. It was like stepping out of the Post Office Tower. I had never felt gravity like that before, never felt so much empty space below my feet. It seemed to be sucking at me, trying to pull me off the rock. All my confidence vanished. I could feel my bowels churn.

What the fuck am I doing up here?

Alex was out of sight, round a corner, sitting on a ledge about 80 ft higher. His voice drifted down. 'Keep climbing. This bit is called the Nose. It's the crux. The hardest bit. Once you've done this, it's easy.'

I glanced to my side. The drop below was horrendous and the rock seemed to be pushing me out, willing me to fall. I felt like an unwelcome guest, that I had no business being there. Every negative thought, every paralysing emotion flooded over me.

I couldn't even get into the school football team, what the hell am I doing up here?

I started shaking, my stomach lurched like a trapped cat.

Why couldn't I have just stuck to hillwalking?

I realised I was panicking and that I had two options. The first was to somehow climb across and up the rock face and maybe I would make it.

Jesus, I'm hundreds of feet off the ground.

The second was to stay where I was until the trembling in my legs shook me off the rock altogether.

This stupid bit of rope won't do a thing, it'll snap and I'll be dead.

I could imagine the jagged rock ripping me apart. I swallowed hard and tried to breathe deeply, certain I was about to throw up. I shouted and swore at Alex for getting me into this, then faced into the rock, curled my trembling fingers round a tiny edge and somehow half-climbed and half-leapt up over the small, sharp holds towards him. Even though he was high above, I moved so fast that I was beside him before I'd had a chance to think about it. Panic is a great thing.

'Well done, that man!' He was calmly puffing a cigar, smiling.

'That's it, you've done it. It's all over now,' he said, gathering in the coils of rope.

'Is that really it?' I was none too sure. We still seemed a long way from safety, perched far too high up the massive rock face of Rannoch Wall.

'Yeah, just a walk off from here. We'll go down Curved Ridge. It's a dawdle.'

There was a very faint trail to the left and we followed it to Curved Ridge, a long, steep spine of rock that led back down the mountain. We sat at the top of it for a while, Alex grinning through the cigar smoke, telling me I had done just fine and laughing when I told him how terrified I had been. He turned and pointed across Rannoch Moor and smiled contentedly, a happy man. The sun was starting to sink behind the summit above us and it cast the mountain's long triangular shadow far across the moor. My pulse slowed down to just under 200 and, for a moment, I forgot how frightened I had been.

While there was still light, we scrambled down the ridge. It is harder than Aonach Eagach and a lot steeper, but compared to what we'd just climbed the holds seemed huge; it was almost like climbing down a ladder. I began to relax, just enough to start enjoying it. We carefully stepped across a ledge above a little waterfall as it toppled down the side of the mountain, then we skittered down a scree slope to a path leading back to the car park.

Thank fuck. At last, all the tension rushed out of my body.

Alex turned and saw my face glowing. 'You look like you enjoyed that?'

'Are you kidding? I was petrified. I knew if I didn't make that move at the Nose my legs would have given out altogether, it was fucking awful.' I grinned.

'Yeah, but you conquered your fear, didn't you? The next time you are on a rock climb, you'll know you can control your fear. Climbing is all about mind control, conquering your fear.'

I thought about this for a while as we walked down the path, past a little cottage and back to where Alex had parked his

Land-Rover. When you have your own business, you have to face up to all sorts of crap. You build it up and then inevitably lose major contracts through no fault of your own. A few weeks before, some faceless accountant's decision in Peterborough to change suppliers overnight had cost us half our storage revenue and 20 per cent of our trucking income. He probably went home that day without giving it any more thought than his morning fart. It was a lot of money that we depended on to stay afloat. That kept me awake at night for weeks. You have to keep going, somehow find new work; there's no point whining.

And, of course, it's never dull running a company in an inner-city area. Some neds used pickaxes to knock a hole through a wall in my store and ransack the place. Another time, a gang stole one of my trucks and used it in a ram-raid. That put the insurance premiums up a bit. Oh, yeah, nearly forgot, we had a couple of armed robberies too. Situations like that are scary.

As we got near the bottom of the mountain, it occurred to me that controlling fear in business couldn't be harder than conquering it on a rock face. This climbing lark could have beneficial side effects.

'So, when do you fancy another route?' Alex asked cheerily, as the last of the daylight slipped behind the hills.

'If you think for a second that I will ever put myself in that position again, that I'll ever go climbing again, you're out of your fucking mind!'

And, of course, he was.

12

ROCK AND ROLL

Ben Lawers

IF YOU ARE A MUSICIAN, YOU NEVER FEEL QUITE RIGHT IF YOU ARE NOT PLAYING in a decent band, and I didn't. For a long time, the nearest I'd been to a stage was pushing Pavarotti's piano around when he played Glasgow, which is not really the same. I particularly fancied playing in a soul band. 'Midnight Hour', 'Soul Man' – all that good stuff. The problem is that semi-pro bands take a huge amount of organising. You have to get the musicians together, which is not an easy job – there are thousands of people who can beat the crap out of a drum kit in their garage or knock a tune out of a guitar in their front room, but relatively few can play with other people in a band. It's playing in time and leaving space which can be tricky.

Running the business was too demanding for me to let the notion of putting a band together even cross my mind, but I really missed standing on a hot stage in front of a couple of hundred sweating people. I was confident I could play gigs in places where *the drink* was an arm's length away, even relax backstage surrounded by gallons of free booze without touching it.

Sometimes, when you are playing in a band, all the sounds merge together and surround you in a warmth you can't get anywhere else; it becomes a living thing. When it happens, the musicians love it; the crowd can hear something is going on and it's those moments that make all the hassle worthwhile.

Then I had a call from a mate who owned a music shop. A customer was looking for a bass player – *hey, hold on, I'm comin'* – so I trotted off to meet him. I preferred playing bass; it was less work than learning guitar parts with all the twiddly bits. The business was busy, but busy in a drive-you-out-of-your-mind kind of way. A little music would help.

The drummer was a great musician, an old has-been like me, and had played with Leo Sayer, or someone similar. I think he also did a stint as a Womble, but he kept quiet about that. We had a female horn player from the Gorbals who really knew her stuff; she'd played with Gary Glitter. She was about to go onstage with him at a packed gig in Glasgow when he pointed to her sax and ordered her to paint it silver. In a voice that could cut steel she told him to fuck off before she wedged it up his arse. He could hardly sing the first song for laughing. The keyboard player was excellent and went on to do world tours with Marianne Faithfull, at one time every schoolboy's fantasy. It was a good little band.

We never made any money out of it – the costs were too high. Hiring all those lights and high-wattage sound equipment didn't come cheap – but it was great fun playing occasional business conferences and university dances. Travis supported us once – it was one of their first gigs and it was obvious they were headed for the big-time. They were slick as silk.

Rory McCann was in the band; a great frontman who is now a Hollywood film star. He is 6 ft 6 in. tall and strong as a Bridgeton bouncer. He got his first acting break in the Scots Porage advertisement – the one where the girls queue to look up his kilt. Rory liked hillwalking and climbing, and one weekend we drove to Ben Lawers in Perthshire. He had borrowed a low-slung sports car and I drove while he sat in the passenger seat with his head sticking up through the open sunroof; he'd do anything for a laugh. It was a freezing, damp and foggy February day, and Ben Lawers was deep in snow. Being a penniless actor, Rory had no 'proper' hillwalking clothes nor Gore-tex jacket; he was wearing an old rugby shirt and a yellow plastic anorak that had been supplied to him when he'd worked as a painter, swaying off the Forth Road Bridge.

I am 6 ft, but had nothing nearly big enough to lend him. He pulled on an old pair of size 14 work boots and we set off. It was a two-hour plod up and we were dripping like Bombay baggage handlers when we eventually stamped our feet on the top. We realised we couldn't stop for more than a few minutes: the sweat that was saturating the inside of his jacket was freezing fast. It was cold, seriously cold. We even had frost in our hair; his eyebrows were thick lines of encrusted snow. We shared a quick flask of hot soup then started heading back down. About halfway, he paused and looked at the steep snow slope below as it vanished into the mist. We couldn't see more than 20 ft ahead.

'Fuck it!' he shouted to me. 'Let's go for it!'

Without hesitation, he jumped on to the hard snow and rocketed off down the slope on his arse, and was immediately swallowed up by the thick mist. He had no ice axe to slow or stop him and no idea of what lay below; it could have been a *Touching the Void*-type cliff. It was so against the accepted rules of hillwalking that I almost pissed myself laughing. Then his excited voice yelled from below.

'Come on, hurry up, it's brilliant!'

Some hillwalkers were watching us and tutting in disapproval. They shook their woolly-hatted heads and wagged their fingers in thick gloves, snug in their latest technical jackets, pointing their regulation-length walkers' ice axes at us.

'Stupid bloody fools. What a stupid thing to do.'

They were right, of course; it was daft, but I looked at them, then listened to McCann's excited, childlike shouts of joy from somewhere below in the fog. Sod it. I jumped into the trench that his arse had cleared and shot down into the white mist until the drop levelled out and we stood up and laughed like school kids.

He was filming a TV series called *The Book Group* when he called and told me that he had hung a photograph of us at the top of Ben Lawers on a wall in one of the scenes they were shooting. 'I play the part of a climber who gets crippled in an avalanche that kills my father. I'm in bed with two beautiful girls – it's brilliant, getting paid for doing that! In the scene, I tell them that the picture is of me and my dad.'

Shit, I'm getting old.

Another time, the band was doing an end-of-term marquee job at Jordanhill College. I had been working all week, rushing around like a scalded cat and had already played a corporate gig at the Marriott earlier that night. It was two in the morning before we went on and I was knackered. It was packed, sauna-hot and draining every last bit of my energy. The place was dripping with sweat – perfect for R'n'B – the students were seriously up for it, every one of them utterly pissed out their heads; a wild night.

A pleasantly plump girl was crammed against the front of the stage just below me and when we blasted into the last song, 'Sweet Home Chicago', she went crazy, lifting her skirt and swaying her ass like a stripper. Then she pulled off her T-shirt, threw her bra into the cheering crowd, jumped onstage and began sashaying around like Tina Turner on snozzle. She leaned in close and shouted something to me, but with all the noise – there were 12 musicians belting it out – I only caught one word: bed.

At last, we finished the song and above all the yelling I asked her what she had said. With the sort of sympathetic look she might have given a weary grandfather, she smiled and said: 'You look like you should be home in your bed.'

13

RIDERS ON THE STORM

Big Six

THERE ARE VAST WIDE-OPEN SPACES IN SCOTLAND THAT ARE LIKE THE OLD West.

When I was a boy, I loved Westerns. The thing that fascinated me about them was the way cowboys stopped for the night below a glorious sunset, threw their saddles on the ground, ate some stew and beans – always beans – then settled down with a blanket pulled over them. They lay there, quietly gazing into the glittering galaxies, watching the stars slowly slip by, then peacefully drifted off to sleep. How great would that be! The freedom of big-sky country! So, when Alex called and suggested we head up north with a couple of his friends to mosey around some really remote hills and sleep out on them, I couldn't say yes fast enough. Especially since no climbing ropes would be involved – I had no intention of putting myself through *that* again.

It was arranged: we were going off to do the famous Big Six. It is a long outing. If you are rounding up Munros – and why wouldn't you be? – you can cheerfully tick off another six elusive summits. They are lazily sprawled around an area often called 'the Last Great Wilderness', and it would be rather odd to describe it as being near anywhere because it isn't. It, eh, wouldn't be a wilderness if it was.

If you look at the map, you will see the little outpost called Garve north-west of Inverness. From there, the A835 forms a circle with the A832, and the huge tract of empty land contained within this is the wilderness. And it is huge. It might have ended up falling victim to the Hydro-Electric Board, but one of the landowners, a Colonel Whitbread, although not reported to have been the hillwalkers' best pal, kept the vandals off with the end of his shotgun. Brilliant, just like the Wild West. *Jes' keep on a-riding, or ah'll fill ya full of lead.* Of course, there are many other mountains in the area – it is so mind-numbingly vast – but these six taken together are the most remote Munros in Scotland and when you have done them, you know they don't come any more isolated.

You really want to do them in good weather. Given the choice, most sane people prefer hillwalking in sunshine, but this tends to be rare as far as the Big Six are concerned. The area has huge amounts of porridge-like bogs and they didn't get that way by being in an arid climate akin to Death Valley. The view from the top of any of these mountains can be life-changing; if you ever have trouble sleeping at night, you only have to recall looking out to the sea and the Summer Isles, and you will slip away like a contented child. The views are among the best in the world, but you do have to walk an awfully long way to see them. Then you have to walk back again. You will not be disturbed at any point in the walk by Japanese tourists posing for snapshots. That is a guarantee.

None of these vistas can be seen from Shenavall bothy, where many hillwalkers stay before or after doing the Big Six, to shorten the long trek. Some of Scotland's bothies are delightful little huts; life-saving sanctuaries in remote, untamed land, a credit to generations of hillwalkers who leave them thoughtfully clean and tidy, with a little supply of firewood and a box of dry matches for the next occupant who might stagger in through the snow and ferocious wind on a dark winter's night.

Not Shenavall, at least not when I saw it. Perhaps it is better now, but at the time it was like the Cholera Arms Hotel. If you know the sweet, sickly stench of mouse piss, then you would be able to recognise the smell seeping from this bothy before you stepped inside. Outside, it looked like General Custer and his cavalry had formed a circle, seen 'the Injuns' and immediately emptied their bowels, as they would. There was a rusting car seat lying in a corner. What retard carried that five miles to the bothy? And another old leather chair that must have been home to a vast colony of insects, which is probably why someone had set fire to it. The place stank like an old barn that had been used as a rest home for geriatric horses. You might want to avoid an overnight stop there – it's far better to sleep out on one of the hills, like a cowboy in the high lonesome, and you don't need any of that Ray Mears extreme survival stuff either.

You also definitely don't want to do this hike in a new pair of boots that you haven't broken in. If you are going to hoof the best part of forty miles – I told you it was a long way – over six massive mountains, it should really be in snug, friendly boots that know your feet well. Since I had now done about 150 Munros, you'd think I'd have known that. You really would have thought so.

Alex and one of his pals, 'Fit Boy Slim', collected me and we met 'Nervous Nigel' at his ranch in Perth. FBS had driven us in his nice warm people-carrier, in which it was possible to sprawl out – Alex had snored contentedly all the way from Glasgow. It was going to be a long drive (it's such a treat when someone else takes the steering wheel) and I was looking forward to a comfortable snooze whilst listening to some chill-out music. FBS, however, had been a bad boy and his wife had not let him work any overtime for almost a year, so he had no money and had failed to insure the car. Nervous Nigel, who worked as a health and safety officer, insisted we transfer to his Audi estate.

I am sure the good people at Audi build highly reliable cars, but German seats are designed for better padded arses than are usually found in the UK. Audis, Mercs and BMWs are all the same. Unless you have a substantial Germanic butt – oversized, well-padded twins wobbling like plump jellies between you and the hard seat – you are in for a tough ride. From a purely posterior point of view, Toyotas are a far more luxurious mode of transportation – their seats being designed with scrawny little Oriental arse-bones in mind. You can travel the length of the UK in a Japanese car without a break, whereas in a German machine, you will feel the pressure of the seat grinding and chewing your bahookie every mile of the way.

We were only an hour late arriving at Nigel's house, but he was one tense *hombre*. No, there was no time for coffee, we had to be on our way. *Now*. NN likes to be on time. His life is dedicated to punctuality. He feels uncomfortable at the slightest change in schedule and you could see his upper lip twitch as we piled into his immaculately tidy car. It seemed a long drive to Inverness, even though he was driving so fast the road funnelled in front of us like a blurred tunnel. It was a warm June morning, but as we glanced at the Cairngorm Mountains flashing by, we could see fresh snow on the summits. We charged over the Kessock Bridge then, after racing past a few petrol tankers, Nigel reluctantly skidded to a halt in front of a little roadside cantina.

We squeezed out, kneaded our saddle-sore rumps then greedily wolfed down ham, eggs and a pot of coffee. We were just about to order a third pot when we noticed a vein pulsing in NN's forehead. We shuffled out as quickly as possible, folded ourselves back into the Audi and roared off again. At last, NN pulled into a little lay-by on the A832 and screamed to a standstill, throwing a cloud of dust and stones into the air. Time to hit the trail.

This was FBS's first day back on the hills and he was as excited as a greyhound in a cattery. Dressed in black, skin-tight Lycra shorts and whippet-thin, he looked like a gypsy's dog, all ribs and dick. His fitness had not waned even though his training routine had been limited to setting up his bike on a frame in the living room and pounding out 8o miles a night under his wife's grim watch. For a full ten months she had seen to it that he went nowhere. It had all seemed innocent enough when the young aerobics instructor from the gym opposite the factory where Slim worked had asked him to teach her the basic skills of rock climbing and, being a helpful sort of chap, he'd been pleased to oblige . . .

I dragged my rucksack from the back of the car and grunted; it was like lifting a full body bag. Cowboys only seem to carry a single blanket rolled up behind their saddle. Then again, this isn't Texas. I was lugging all the stuff you are supposed to carry when going anywhere in the Scottish hills: waterproofs, a warm fleece, base and mid-layers, a hat of some sort, gloves; a warm sleeping bag with a separate rainproof cover called a bivvy bag, a compass and Leki walking-sticks, a little stove, fuel and a map. I had far too much food, but we'd be at least a day's walk from the nearest general store, so hopefully I wouldn't starve to death.

As we set off, I worried for a moment about my new boots. No matter what I buy, I have trouble getting a decent fit. One foot is one size and the other is, well, another. I have thought of making up a pair of two boots of different sizes when the sales assistant isn't looking, but the local Sunday School got hold of me when I was a child and I just couldn't do it. Apart from that, I always buy my stuff from Alex's shop and he'd notice right away.

It doesn't matter what I wear, I am always going to have a festival of trouble with my feet. I've worn the lot, but they all end up the same. The manufacturers make their boots perfectly, but their carefully selected lasts and the toil of little bespectacled cobblers with tiny nails held in their lips count for nothing. Their craftsmanship is a lost cause on my feet. They might as well be called Blisterers, Kripplers and Skinners and Agonisers. I've studied all the reviews in *Trail*, worn great furrows in my carpets trying them on at home, sometimes for weeks on end (Alex is very understanding that way), had my feet measured and remeasured, state-of-the-art insoles fitted, but always end up buying a pair too small or large that grind my heels to raw flesh. Eventually, I grow calluses in the right places for each new pair, but that takes a lot of painful miles spread over weeks.

Fit Boy Slim could hardly contain himself as we began walking on the rough track inland towards the first hill of the walk, Beinn a' Chlaidheimh, which apparently means 'hill of the sword'. My boots were bloody killing me; there was a sharp pain eating at my heels. Rather like a sword cut, in fact. Within an hour, I was thinking about changing my name to Hopalong. FBS was glowing with the anticipation of two days in the hills and he took up the front of our little posse. The last thing I wanted to do was fall behind and end up alone, wandering about like a fart in a trance in the Great Wilderness, so I hurried along in his tracks.

> Fit Boy Slim had missed the mountains during his long months of purgatory. Looking back now, an older and wiser man, he should have seen the signs. As they had prepared for the climbing lesson, his pulse had quickened when she had lifted her arms and tilted her pelvis slightly upward so he could help her tighten the climbing harness, but he'd put that down to the natural apprehension any conscientious instructor would feel when teaching a beginner. Sure, her waist was wonderfully slim, his wife had been letting herself go just a little in recent years and . . . he'd brushed the thought from his consciousness.

As we walked up and over Beinn a' Chlaid . . . whatever the hell it was called, we kept glancing east to see what the weather was doing. Plenty. A huge cauldron of angry black clouds was churning on the other side of the country, but we seemed to be on the edge of it. There was a helluva lot of rain out there. It looked like there was a storm a-brewing, a humdinger. It began pouring down through a huge rainbow about five miles away, but the sky above us was blue with just the odd puffy cloud. There was no wind, which was a good sign (if you are about to get dumped on by torrential rain, wind often blasts you first), and the view westward towards the coast was clear. It looked as if we might just get lucky.

By the time we had wandered up and over two Munros, Chlaid whatever and Sgurr Ban, which is the $5 name for 'white peak', it was getting late, so we decided to throw down our bedrolls just below the summit of a mountain called Mullach Coire Mhic Fhearchair, which has something to do with a guy called Farquhar. There are many Farquhars living in Edinburgh's Morningside apartments, sipping brandy and reading *The Scotsman*; in Glasgow, if you're called Farquhar, you're either good with your fists or fast on your feet.

I often wonder what happened to the unsuspecting kids who were given quaint names by their hippy parents back in the '60s. I knew entire communes of them; the String Band had followers who trawled libraries of mythology for weird and wonderful appellations to bestow upon the fruits of their loins. Frey, Astral, Moonbeam: somehow I can't see them today, as adults, in dusty dungarees, wearing those steel toe-capped boots all the builders use, slouching into some smoky pub in Govan after a day on the construction site and introducing themselves with a gnarly handshake to the clientele. Mind you, at least they wouldn't pee on the floor, like a removal man I knew – there was no chance he was going to leave an unguarded pint in *that* saloon.

Nervous Nigel dreaded sleeping on the ground, but he would put up with almost anything to tick off these hills. He didn't like insects – 'wee beasties', he called them. Like me, Nigel had never slept on a hill before, even though he'd climbed all but a few of the Munros. So it was with some excitement that I finally dropped my bulging saddlebag on the ground and tried to reset the bones in my shoulders back to a normal position, then unfolded my bedroll and felt the ground for a dry spot without stones that would poke into me all night.

The glorious weeks of summer had flashed by in a daze of tender delights. At every opportunity, they would seek out new climbs then make love, sometimes in wild celebration of a desperately hard route conquered, their climbing hardware clanking frantically; or gently on a cliff top beneath the golden glow of the setting sun, warm in gentle contemplation of the forbidden hours they'd shared together. But each meeting at the dark end of the street was bringing them closer to that fateful night where the inevitable awaited . . .

Alex lit a stove and fired up some coffee in a tin pot. We sat looking over the hills to the western sea, where we could see the huge Cuillin Ridge thrusting out of the ocean like shark's teeth. The sun slipped gently beyond the horizon, the eastern clouds had gone; it was turning into a beautiful night. It was cold, a dry cold, with not a breath of wind and a sunburst sky all around. No flesh-eating midges, just absolute silence in this huge, empty land.

All very well, but would I be able to sleep? I was none too sure. As anyone who has run a company will know, sleep can be difficult enough at home in your own cosy bed. When you have your own business, there is plenty to keep you wide awake as the demons of darkness dance around your head. I was used to insomnia, but apprehensive about lying awake all night, since I still had a great many miles to cover the next day. Alex shook his rucksack and realised he'd forgotten his bivvy bag. He grinned – *shucks, it don't make no neverminds* – then snuggled down into his sleeping bag and, five minutes later, was fast asleep. Within ten minutes, a thin coating of white frost had covered his bag. It was going to be a cold night up here.

BBC Scotland's most-loved forecaster, Heather the Weather, would have chosen a more scholarly word, but Baltic was the one we used. Really cold, but beautiful. FBS, a veteran of such outings, had staked his claim to a little piece of flat land and advised us to jump up and down to get really warm, then leap into our bags. I don't remember big John Wayne doing that as he settled down beneath the outstretched arms of cactus plants.

NN warily eyed the grass for critters and pulled his bag tightly around him. As I lay in my bag just below the top of Farquhar's mountain, I felt warm (the extra weight had been worth it) and looked at the sky, which held its reddish-golden glow just above the horizon all night. I know this because, while Alex and FBS slept like well-fed cats, I tossed and turned and could not drop off. Neither could NN, who was lying silently awake about five yards away, convinced he was about to be eaten by creepy-crawlies or bitten by rattlers.

I stared deep into the night sky, watching little meteor trails and far-off satellites racing high above on unknown missions until the glow of sunrise crept up behind the peaks on the other side of the country. For a short time, it was possible to see the last colours of sunset and the first of sunrise mirror one another on opposite coasts. I looked up at the black sky between the twin horizons: a star-filled painting in a golden frame. Even if I was going to be totally knackered in the morning, I thought, it was worth lying awake all night on a mountain in this empty place.

> FBS slept soundly for the first time since that fateful night last year. At last, it was behind him. Had they paused, breathed deeply, perhaps listened to Ry Cooder's lonesome guitar, they would have thought about what they were doing, realised this was the way they'd make a broken heart. But it was too late; the passions of the fit are strong . . .

Morning. I had a good scratch, rubbed my eyes and looked at the already blue sky. It was going to be a perfect day. We'd knocked it off! Fit Boy Slim, Nervous Nigel and I quickly nipped up the short distance to the top of a mountain – *yeah, another Munro, tick!* – while Alex rustled up beans and sausages. Sure, we were tired, and I didn't have the courage to take off my socks to see what was happening to my heels, but the view was so stunning I was able to ignore the pain. It was just a flesh wound.

After our open-air breakfast, we all set off again, taking a break about four hours later at the top of another mountain (I can't recollect what it was called), looking over the edge into the vast corral below while we scoffed some more grub; after all, we had plenty. The pain in my feet was getting worse; they were stinging with each hirpling step, and we still had hours of walking ahead of us. Oh well.

The weather was so good and the views so stunning that I forgot all about my feet and finally reached the last Munro of the six, called the Big Red Stack, which means Ruadh Stac Mor. We settled down for a long rest, the sun beaming down on us. Alex and FBS had done these hills before, but they had been shrouded in thick mist; it was actually quite endearing to see how excited they were now they were able to see the view.

After several coffees and more food, we walked down – FBS skipping ahead – paddled through a river, plodded through an acre or so of thick peat swamp and wandered into the empty Shenavall bothy. Since we were all working the next day, we had to keep hoofing it back to Nervous Nigel's car. It was ten o'clock at night when I finally took off my boots with a gasp of relief. My socks were soaked in blood. I remembered my favourite line from a cowboy movie I saw as a kid – 'ah got the death rattle in ma gullet an' ahm sinkin' fast'. I'd live.

Slim's wife had decided not to tell him that her long stretch on night shift was now at an end; she would surprise him by coming home early. Some tequila, perhaps a joint of the special grass he liked so much. It would be like old times when they'd first met in her *pueblocito*, her home village so far from this cold land. She'd hurried to the door of their little flat, happy to see that the light was on inside. He'd be so pleased to see her . . .

It was another long, stiff drive back to Perth down the dark A9 and, just to ensure a cheery journey, NN insisted on silence, no heating and hypothermia-inducing open windows in case he fell asleep in the saddle. You'd have thought the unyielding Audi seats would have been enough. But it had been a fabulous trip.

Where seldom was heard a discouraging word.

Must do it again soon. I'll wear old boots, though.

And the skies are not cloudy all day.

14

GOD ONLY KNOWS

New Zealand

THE BUSINESS WAS DOING MUCH BETTER. I'D SNARED A CONTRACT WITH Christie's, the auctioneers, had recruited some excellent staff, moved into a bigger warehouse and we were working very hard to build a highly professional moving company. The telephones were busy except during January, when the industry was always at its quietest. I used to hate the long, dark nights of winter, so one year I flew to New Zealand to meet up with Mickey, my old drummer pal, who was living in Wellington. I was looking forward to winter sun, doing some hillwalking with him at Lake Taupo and Queenstown, and sitting in with his band at a couple of gigs. He had a family now, so he didn't open the first can of the day until almost six o'clock; apart from that, he'd hardly changed – he was still crazy.

Yes, of course. I'd only been there two nights before I joined him in his nightly glug – you really would have thought I'd have learned by now. I hadn't been near *the drink* for years and thought I had lost any desire, but it had happened quite accidentally. I had stopped in a pub to say goodbye to some of my staff and one of the girls had got two glasses mixed up and handed me what she thought was an orange juice. It was, but full of vodka. One taste, that same old mentality: one drink made you feel good, therefore two will make you feel twice as good.

The thing is, to stay sober you need to be on your guard all the time and that becomes wearisome. You get tired always being the designated driver; tired that everyone else seems to be able to have a good time without stepping across the line from fun to lunacy. It seems that you are always the one who can't just chill with a few friends and some beers. *Why can't you just relax?* You get so damn tired of always taking life too seriously and slowly find yourself chipping away at the defences you've built to stop yourself stretching out and having a few.

And when the first one goes down, it's like meeting up with an old friend. *Where have you been all these years?* You feel like yourself again, not the boring fart you thought you'd become. You manage to stick to a couple and, *hey, that wasn't so bad, was it?* You're older now, you can control it. You remember all the things you like about it, you feel the coiled spring inside ease off, you feel new confidence; you can have a social drink. You are more relaxed during the day, find yourself looking forward to dusk, knowing you will be able to enjoy a drink or two – only a couple – and unwind . . .

Mickey and I drank our way around the North and South islands. On the flight home, I had got back into the way of it and downed a constant stream of gin and tonic on the plane. It was all they had. It would do, it was alcohol. Doubles, of course. When the plane juddered to a halt at Heathrow, I thought I needed an MRI, my head was pounding like a ship's engine. By the time I got back to Glasgow, I was so hung over I just wanted to slink into bed in a dark room instead of enjoying being with my two teenage sons again. As soon as I saw them, all the reasons for stopping came back to me and I quit again.

I wasn't born to lose you.

15

CHILDREN OF THE REVOLUTION
Rock gyms and catwalk climbers

ALEX AND I HAD BEEN HILLWALKING SOMEWHERE NORTH OF FORT WILLIAM, ONE of the Munros there, I can't remember which. They are all brilliant – even ones the books describe as big, boring plods. It was one of those easy days just wandering in the hills, smoothing out the kinks that the working week had pounded deep into our muscles. *Lazy Sunday afternoon.* We had stopped on the road back for something to eat in the 'Starving Bastard' restaurant (they don't actually call it that, but we do, because, well, you have to be). I'm not a fussy eater – I've never been sophisticated enough to appreciate the joys of French cuisine, that whole peasants-dying-of-starvation thing, cooking every last scrap of the animal, every organ from its toes to its teeth – face, arse, balls, everything – the egg and chips they served up were just fine.

As we burped home, Alex chatted about one of his favourite subjects: Tolkien and *The Lord of the Rings*. This was long before the Hollywood blockbuster. In the '60s and early '70s, the book had been a huge favourite of acid freaks. Robert Plant loved it – given the chance, he would ramble on about how in the darkest depths of Mordor, he'd met a girl so fair, but Gollum crept up and slipped away with her. *Hu-uur.* Like, bummer, man. Unfortunately, the whole thing had kind of passed me by. Maybe I'd been just a little *too* stoned.

Alex is passionate about Tolkien and was telling me how the writer believed he was recalling past lives and that Middle-earth had really existed. If it had, it wasn't my time or place – even in my most zonked-out hippy days, I'd never been able to read *LotR*. I know I've been to a lot of places and there's a lot of places I know I've been, but Middle-earth isn't one of them. I hadn't been there in a previous incarnation, although as I listened to Alex, I thought that perhaps he had. He was glowing as he talked and the idea of Westernesse and the Inklings resonated in me: the idea that there is something just out of reach that you can't quite explain. When you gaze to the west from the top of a Munro, you often feel a strong pull, a longing to be *over there*. Just where you don't know. It's the sensation I'd had all those years ago when I used to look up from the Hangover Hotel. *I still haven't found what I'm looking for.*

I dozed as Alex quoted long sections. When his children were young, he'd never read them nursery rhymes; they gently drifted off to sleep with mental images of Frodo and Gandalf. It is really nice to see someone gain so much enjoyment from a book. It was a very pleasant drive beside Loch Lomond while he talked of elves, intrigue and the power of the ring. Then he said something that made me think he'd really lost the plot.

'I'm going to open a climbing wall. Me and my brother-in-law and another guy who sells Mars bars for a living. We're renting an old church and we're going to build a climbing wall.'

'A climbing wall? Do you reckon you'll be able to make it pay? I mean, climbers are notoriously tight, are they not?'

This was the thing – there has always been a sort of northern ethos among climbers, the feeling that you were soft if you paid for anything unless you absolutely had to. When British climbers began making mass invasions on Chamonix in the '60s and '70s, roaring into town on oily, rusting motorbikes and clapped-out Post Office vans, the local community didn't know what had hit them. These unwashed ruffians, sleeping in tents in a field, pissing on the grass, *merde* everywhere. They had discovered that an ancient French law, from the time of the revolution, prohibited prosecution of anyone caught stealing food for their own consumption. *Bloody heck!* They rolled up their sleeves, stretched their fingers, pulled on their baggy shoplifting jerseys, then swarmed into the village shops and set about liberating all the cheese, bread and milk they could get their hands on. *The boys are back in town.* They were like modern-day locusts.

In Yosemite National Park, climbers used to prowl around the restaurants and hoover up anything that Mom, Pop and the little ones left on their plates, often while they were still sitting at the table. Junior would look up from his meatloaf and mashed potatoes straight into the eager bloodshot eyes of a bearded hobo whose waiting hands were still cut and caked with climbing chalk after a desperate three-day ascent of El Cap. They were worse than bears: you could lock up your food where Yogi couldn't reach it, but these guys saw every plate as fair game. I couldn't imagine how characters like that would ever pay money to climb; besides, there was a climbing wall at the Kelvin Hall and it was usually deserted. When it wasn't, the guys using it had found some way of sneaking in without coughing up the tiny admission charge.

'Yeah, but it's crap. Wait till you see this thing. It's going to be unbelievable. It takes up the whole of the inside of the church. We've flogged the pews and we'll build these artificial climbing walls. People can train indoors all year round. It will be brilliant!'

'Are you sure about this, Alex? You really think you can make this pay?'

It was great to see him so enthusiastic and he disappeared for months. Now and then, he would drop by for a quick coffee, usually about one in the morning – *sorry, did I get you out of bed?* He was always buzzing with excitement, concrete dust in his hair, hands covered with sticky resin or paint. He told me he was putting a sound system into the church so I gave him two huge battered speaker cabs that had been blocking out the light in my garage. One Sunday night he came across to my house, his eyes sparkling.

'We've got one of the walls ready! Come on over and you can try it. See what you think.'

I'd just got back from hillwalking and was about to drop into a hot foaming bath, but this sounded good so I squeezed into his Land-Rover, pushing aside tins of paint, ladders and bags of concrete. You can get a lot in a Land-Rover when the seats are ripped out.

After that day with Alex on the Bookle, I'd gradually done more rock climbing. Oh, it starts innocently enough: you go to a little cliff or other, just for a little taste, you say you won't get hooked like all the others, but once you have learned how a rope works, and things like that, it creeps up on you and before you know it you're addicted. You fall a couple of times and realise that you can trust the system: your climbing partner will hold you just fine. Really, the only fall I've had that still wakes me from a deep sleep was not from a cliff. While I was touring America with the ISB, I'd got friendly with Rory Gallagher. After we'd enjoyed a three-hour backstage drinking session, he'd invited me onstage at a gig in Long Island to jam with him and his band – it was like being asked to play in a Cup final at Hampden. He handed me his guitar while he played slide on his white Telecaster. Somewhere around the 12th bar, I stepped backwards and toppled over a monitor speaker into the crowd. Rory couldn't stop laughing. Ever since, I've been tormented by the thought of how close I'd come to wrecking his beloved old sunburst Strat. Somehow, lobbing off a rock face on the end of a climbing rope has seemed, by comparison, fairly minor.

Climbing also seemed to be helping me run the business.

When you are climbing, you have to set yourself little objectives. If you look at a climb in its entirety, it will seem impossible – you will never be able to get up it – so you break it down into little sections. You concentrate on getting your arse up one little bit, you tell yourself if you can climb that part of the rock just up to the next ledge, then you can sort the rest out later. When you get there, you realise it wasn't so bad and you look for the next series of moves you have to make. Your self-confidence grows. You can do this.

So off we trotted. The inside of the church in Govan was still a building site, but one wall was built out like an overhanging cliff using some sort of resinous material, similar to real rock, which, of course, was exactly what it was supposed to be like. Little holds were bolted all over it. Of course, these climbing walls are everywhere now, they even used them in *Gladiators*, that bizarre prime-time TV programme that gave us those unforgettable 'pugil' sticks and the bikini-clad models who battered each other with them, their arses wobbling like jellyfish on Red Bull.

Nowadays, if you go into any theme park, like Universal or Busch Gardens in Florida, you'll find mini-walls; five bucks a climb or whatever they charge. But that night in Glasgow was the first time I had seen a proper indoor climbing wall, what the Americans call rock gyms. Alex locked the large double doors to keep out any of the 'Pure Mental Govan Young Team', who might be looking for someone to head-butt, turned on a CD player and suddenly 'Brown Sugar' was blasting out of the speakers.

It was great fun. And he was right, which has pleased his bank manager. Indoor climbing walls have become a huge success; there are similar ones all over Britain. Within a few years of opening, Glasgow Climbing Centre, or 'the Wall' as most people called it, had enrolled over 10,000 members, a staggering number, most of whom had never tried climbing before. When you realise that the two indoor climbing walls in Glasgow and

Edinburgh alone have more members than all the formal climbing clubs in Britain combined, you get an idea of how many people have taken up the sport in the last ten years.

As a result, climbing has changed completely. Before climbing walls became fashionable, most climbers reckoned that training in any structured way was for *poofs* – you got fit by walking *t' tha' cliff, lad*, drilling metal rivets into ships, working *down pit*, or sawing rough timber every day on building sites. It was the preserve of the beard, the cloth cap, the hacking, phlegm-rich bark of Woodbine cigarettes. Climbers did press-ups on the sawdust floor of the pub with someone on their back and drank at least 10 pints a night; they won strength competitions, doing finger pull-ups on 6-in. nails or one-arm chin-ups from the rafters. It was about communal vomit sessions, fearsome punch-ups that were laughed about next day, dossing on dirt floors amid discarded whisky bottles or trying to climb routes in the pissing rain.

The old-style climbers took pride in being tough. Some, such as Doug Scott or Chris Bonington, climbed their way to international fame and a knighthood. Doug Scott looked like a typical hippy until a relatively late age – headband, shoulder-length hair and John Lennon glasses – which disguised his gruffness, immense strength and single-minded determination, which he needed on the massive Himalayan climbs of the day. Scott and Bonington once fought an epic eight-day battle in the Karakoram, crawling down a mountain called the Ogre with two broken legs and several fractured ribs between them. Oh, and Bonington had pneumonia too. Eight days of unimaginable pain. Scott simply shrugged and called it 'a bit of a bad do'.

There were plenty of unknown climbers who loved to try to imitate the hardest of them all, the legendary Don Whillans. The former plumber had survived desperate battles with Alpine storms that would have killed most climbers and was a master of the one-liner. No matter how close he was to the top of a climb, if he saw that horrendous weather conditions were likely to kill someone, he'd quietly set up an abseil down to the door of the nearest pub, grunting, 'I don't mind fighting my way out of trouble, but I'm fucked if I'm going to fight my way into it.' He was a hard nut – if someone was stupid enough to mess about with him or, worse, steal his beer, Whillans would recount what had happened next by simply saying 'and then I hit 'im'. That had always ended it. Even when *the drink* had made him heavily overweight, he could still out-climb almost anyone else, although it all caught up with him when he died of a heart attack aged only 52.

If someone tried to impress Don or anyone else in the pub by bragging, they were soon forced to prove it or bugger off forever, as one guy discovered when he declared a steep cliff in the Lake District so easy that he could climb it 'wearing boxing gloves and roller skates'. Picture that. So he was put to the test and actually succeeded, although as a Yorkshireman who witnessed this unparalleled act of stupidity/bravado grunted, 'Aye, but he was on a bloody top rope.' Which meant that if he fell, he would have been, in theory, safe from death.

I am so glad most of that shit had gone when I got into climbing.

Indoor climbing walls provide an all-weather, all-season environment for climbers to train to exceptional standards because they are working the exact muscles and using the precise techniques required for climbing. Many people train five nights a week and become superb athletes. There is no snobbery or elitism – climbing gyms are open to all, everyone climbs to their own degree of difficulty and, one of the biggest changes of all, there is now a huge number of female climbers. Girls who take up climbing often quickly progress to difficult routes because they learn to use their feet far sooner than their hard-muscled boyfriends who instinctively rely on arm strength. The guys are getting all testosteroned up, using brute force to pull up on big holds, called *jugs*, while their lithe girlfriends, with limited upper-body strength, suddenly climb straight past them because they rely on balance and footwork. Many people are content to use the gyms for a full-body workout; the climbing magazines have not been slow to notice that regular training quickly carves superbly toned bodies and their pages are filled with photographs of scantily clad female climbers who would put most James Bond girls to shame.

They are also very safe places to learn how to climb and use the equipment, and no one has ever been stuck freezing their gonads off all night on a climbing wall, although one of the Glasgow instructors, Neil McGeachy, managed to get locked in one night after falling asleep in the staffroom. He had a bit of explaining to do when the cops caught him abseiling out of the church tower at two in the morning. You can climb the height of the Matterhorn and be home in time for a hot bath and a pizza. At the same time. Pizza in the bath on a winter night. Joy of joys.

In Spain, Italy and France, there are even specially equipped cliffs dedicated to 'sport' climbing, where children can learn while their older brothers and sisters scale seemingly impossible overhanging rock in glorious sunshine. This is far safer and much less macho than old-fashioned climbing, which infuriates some diehards; one well-known writer calls it 'Continental pap'. They *want* climbing to be dangerous, and splutter incoherently over their black-pudding suppers and pints of bitter at the mere suggestion similar areas might be developed in Britain.

Many new climbers have no desire to slog up the old, often scrappy, mountain routes, especially in pissing rain – why should they? – and as a result, some of the old generation do not consider them proper climbers, even though the youngsters can climb far harder routes than they ever could.

The times they are a-changing.

16

LET'S WORK TOGETHER

Ring of Kerry, Eire

I WAS DETERMINED TO MAKE THE REMOVAL BUSINESS AS SUCCESSFUL AS possible. I used to lie in bed at night staring at the ceiling, desperately trying to come up with ways of staying ahead of the competition by offering services that they didn't: we were one of the first moving companies in the UK to be fully computerised – I had commissioned software experts to develop van-scheduling programmes at least ten years before anyone else; as far as I know, we were the only company in Scotland to employ female packers; we invested in all sorts of specialised packing materials and equipment. I was constantly trying to figure out new angles. It was a busy time. I only realised recently that there are hardly any TV programmes from the mid-'80s to the '90s that I recognise. I also missed all that Tenpole Tudor and A Flock of Seagulls music, so there were other benefits too.

One of the things I did to give the business a more professional image, make some contacts and generally learn more about what is a very large worldwide industry was join the national trade association, which entailed going along to monthly meetings. There were many hard-working men at these gatherings; most of them had started as van boys and had forgotten more about running a moving business than I would ever learn, but, without being unkind, they were more at home with oily rags and spanners than laptops. Somebody had to take detailed minutes and I could do that as easily as they could turn a torque wrench, whatever that is. They knew how to change a diesel injector; I didn't even know what one looked like – but I could spell it. I was hardly in the door when they asked me to be secretary.

A couple of years later, I was elected chairman of the Scottish area and, soon after, was invited to the national headquarters in London to join a management committee that was working on completely restructuring the century-old association. They flew me down regularly, every few weeks, sometimes for meetings that would last only a few hours.

When you are a pro musician, you learn very early that appearance is everything: if you look as though you know what you are doing and you play with confidence you can fool most of the people all of the time. I've been in bands with guys who could play in the wrong key with utter panache, myself included. And so I adapted this dubious skill to committee life.

If you hadn't memorised the reams of minutiae that you needed to know, the next best thing was to stare very intently at the sheaf of documents in front of you on the polished mahogany table, listen, utter not a word, but nod like a Victorian headmaster as though deep in thought. The most important thing was to look well ahead on the agenda, thus gaining a head start on everyone else, and figure out just one relevant thing to say; rack your brains for a vital point that, hopefully, hadn't occurred to anyone else.

It's like a good guitar solo: far better to play a short, well-structured break – Jeff Beck's 'Hi Ho Silver Lining' is the perfect example – than any number of motorbike solos from the '70s. You know the ones: they start low and rev up to a load of screaming and wailing. If you make only one crisp point, they'll remember you and not think the cost of your airfare a waste of money. Most people on committees love the sound of their own voices – let them hog the stage until you are ready for the spotlight. It's easy.

Through the trade association, I met a guy who had helped start a removers' cooperative and I had joined it. This had grown from small beginnings to become the huge Britannia Movers International Group. Each member retained their company's individual identity, but, by working together, could at last get a foothold in the huge corporate moving markets previously controlled by companies like Pickfords.

Membership of Britannia was becoming very prestigious – things were definitely improving – and I went over to Ireland with them to cycle round a thing called the Ring of Kerry. It was one of those let's-get-together-and-bond type of things that many people use as an excuse to get pissed witless. I stayed sober. I spent the weekend getting to know as many members as I could, which proved to be very helpful; these guys often needed consignments delivered to Scotland and from then on I never had a van returning empty from the south. There were also some specialised movers in the group who sent trucks to the Continent; I quickly began working closely with them and soon had deliveries leaving my warehouse for the furthest corners of Europe. It all helped.

Kerry is like the west coast of Scotland: picturesque with the occasional little village and quaint pubs that always have the thud of a bodhrán and the cheery sound of the fiddle; a very beautiful part of the world. You meet folk who have gone there for a holiday and never left, like the young couple from Amsterdam who had set up a coffee shop miles from anywhere, happily serving up cake and ice cream to cyclists doing the Ring. They seemed very content, had given birth to a little Irish baby and had almost totally forgotten that cities existed, which would be easy in the perfect sunshine we enjoyed.

Many of the moving-company owners were from London and the Midlands, and they raved about how quiet and peaceful the little narrow roads were. I didn't want to disillusion them. Every five minutes, another tourist coach or line of cars would charge by, overtaking us in a cloud of exhaust fumes. Compared to hundreds of equally beautiful parts of Scotland, the Ring of Kerry can be like a motorway; these guys were so used to living amid noise and traffic, it seemed as deserted as the Mohave Desert. You have to admire their tolerance, the way they can live in a permanent crowd, spending hours travelling to and from work every day. It amazes me that mental hospitals do not have a permanent fleet of padded trucks collecting new drooling patients from the London Underground.

Kerry is lovely, but this was before the Good Friday Agreement and all along the roadside were memorials to fallen IRA members, reminding us we were in another country. After a few pleasant hours pedalling, we stopped at a car park, high above the sparkling ocean. We stretched our arms and sipped energy drinks as the photographer who'd been sent by the trade press to cover the event gathered all 50 of us in a line, then calmly unfurled a massive Union Jack with the word 'Britannia' plastered across it. He gave a corner to the guy at each end of the row and told him to hold it up where it could be seen for the shot.

What had been a merry little car park full of happy tourists suddenly cleared. Just beside us was one of those old guys dressed in welly boots, waistcoat, felt hat, old trousers tied at the knees, posing beside a donkey for anyone who wanted a genuine picture of the *ould coun-tray*. His watery eyes widened when he saw the huge flag and he raced to and fro gathering up his merchandise – linen tea towels, assorted souvenirs and CDs of Irish rebel songs – then dragged the animal clear, muttering, 'Oh, Jaysus fook.'

'That's it, big smile guys. Just spread out a little more. Can you pull the flag a bit higher?'

I gulped. The photographer was from Kent and obviously had no idea of the offence he was causing in the heart of Republican territory. It was like someone marching into the Apollo in Harlem wearing a KKK outfit.

'Just take the bloody picture,' I shouted, 'and you better stick that flag up your arse while you're at it.'

'Why . . . what's your problem, Jock? You Scots are all the same, still can't get over us winning the World Cup . . .'

'See that glint up the hill, there? That's a telescopic sight.'

17

GIMME SHELTER

Cold moonlight, ancient stars

LIKE I DID, MOST HILLWALKERS EAGERLY RUSH ROUND ALL THE MUNROS WITHIN easy reach of their homes and then realise with some dismay that they have to do a vast amount of driving to reach the rest. This involves overnight stays, for which there are a number of choices. You can doss in the car – one guy I know, who is well over 6 ft, seemed to manage it with no ill effects, which amazes me, since he just had a little Polo. A well-known climber called Mick Fowler, who was a taxman living in London, used to drive up to the Northern Highlands on a Friday straight from work, kip for a couple of hours in the back seat, climb all weekend without ever troubling a bed, then race back in time for a doubtlessly bright and breezy start at the office on Monday morning. It is a miracle he didn't leave a trail of motorway carnage in his wake.

A pal of mine who was a career roadie regularly used to put in the same kind of driving hours behind the wheel of a 20-ton truck. He'd roll the gear up the ramps, lock it down and take the first of several swift snorts of cocaine, slip on his Ray-Bans (it was the '70s), then pull out into the fast lane. The sunglasses were to shield his eyes from oncoming headlights. This, he felt, was the cause of motorway fatigue and not the fact that he'd been humping amps and twiddling knobs for 18 hours without a break. He worked for all sorts of bands, started with the String Band at 17 and travelled the world with Zeppelin, The Stranglers, The Who, Floyd, Marley, any name you know.

When he was touring with Little Feat, they had a night off in Dallas, Texas. Oh, yeah. *Lord take me downtown, I'm just lookin' for some tush.* The four things they did on nights off were:

1) find a Miss Wet T-shirt competition
2) do some weed, whites and wine
3) have it off with the winner of the competition
4) snort a heap of cocaine

One night, he hoovered up so much that the left side of his face dropped 'like an old witch's tit' (his expression). His eyes, mouth, everything; he could barely speak. He was rushed, drooling, to hospital, his hooter still liberally caked with white powder. He thought he'd had a stroke. The paralysis didn't ease off for a day or so, and it gave him a fright, but still he drove that night. *Had my head stoved in but I'm still on my feet and I'm willing.* If he'd been pulled over for a routine check, God only knows what a motorway cop would have thought when he saw his face.

There are a lot of narrow road and motorway miles involved in getting round the Munros. If you ever see a convoy of trucks looming up behind you in the early hours of the morning, and they are thick with dirt with less than subtle messages from fans written all over them, you will be looking at a rock and roll band's road crew on the move. It's best to stay clear. Especially if the drivers are wearing Ray-Bans.

If you are not too financially challenged or just incorrigibly miserable, you can buy a bed for the night in a youth hostel, by all accounts much improved since the days of mandatory chores. So I'm told. This wouldn't apply to the very remote

Loch Ossian Hostel, at least when I visited it with Alex and Nervous Nigel. We were on a trip to the Munros nearby and had to catch one of the few daily trains to Corrour Halt station, the nearest point of access to Loch Ossian. Nigel and I were waiting on the platform at Tyndrum, but Alex was late as usual – he just had to have another coffee down in the village.

The only reason we managed to catch the train, and I swear this is true, is because Nervous Nigel stood on the tracks with his hands up in front of the engine while Alex sauntered the last 50 yards to the platform. Nigel had planned to do these Munros *today* and nothing, *nothing*, was going to interrupt his schedule. If this had been anywhere but Scotland, he would have become a long, red smear on the rails. The driver just smiled.

Unlike the warden at the youth hostel. The wind was blowing a hoolie as we walked down towards the loch and reached the hostel. We doubted anyone would mind if we popped in to make a quick cup of tea, especially since NN had an official YHA membership card in his pocket. The warden was German and young, but of the old school. Rigid Teutonic blood throbbed in his veins. He stood to attention, stiffly refusing to let us in, waving us away – 'Zis is for zee guests only!' When we sheltered behind an old hut and lit our little stove, his eyes almost exploded out of his head. 'You must go. *Now!* You must not make zee brew here. Zis is private!'

Highland guest houses are usually very cheap and there are thousands of them, although they're often owned by Essex ex-pats who cashed in on the London property boom and think that curried beans and canned tomatoes are the heart of all good breakfasts. The ones I have stayed in have never been as good as basic bed and breakfast homes in New Zealand, but not as bad as I am told they can be in some mountain regions of the world where the turds from yesterday's guests are often used to fertilise your salad. Just when you thought it was safe to eat the lettuce.

I like staying in hotels, even though in my touring days I sometimes did a spot of reverse decoration on some of the rooms,

121

as one does. Ah, *the drink*. I even worked in a couple before I joined the ISB; one particularly lively place in London, often frequented by members of the Royal family, had a butcher who hosted live sex shows in the kitchen every Sunday afternoon.

Small Scottish hotels can be very pleasant, but the big enemy is dampness: if you can find a place that doesn't have moss on the walls, isn't smelling of mildew, has a shower that works and no fungus sprouting around the toilet, you have knocked it off. Some of them are a real labour of love on the part of the owners. There is one not far from Aviemore which is filled with charming prints, lovingly hand-sewn lace, inviting plump armchairs arranged comfortably around thoughtfully stocked bookcases with fragrant pot-pourri and delicately embroidered bedspreads. Americans would love it. Except for one thing.

The main pipe to the sewage system, for some inexplicable reason, runs right along the dining-room ceiling. Some architect must have had a very strange sense of humour. Just as you are setting yourself up for an energetic day in the hills, savouring your beautifully poached eggs, fried tomato and bacon, someone upstairs will flush away their morning dookie, blissfully unaware as they pull the chain that the diners below can hear the torrent of water crashing down the pipes just above their heads. It's an interesting start to the day.

Then there is camping.

It can be an awful faff, dragging around a tent and all the shit you need to get by for a night or two – sleeping bag, stove, food, pots, all that crap – but Scotland is a wonderful place to camp in the wild, especially below the most remote Munros. Nervous Nigel always worried about being wakened by a pitchfork up his arse, and I am sure the organised campsites he preferred have their charms, though, personally, I find the sound of snoring, farting and humping a few feet away in too-nearby tents as pleasant as piles – the exception, of course, being those couples who enjoy loud speech-play throughout their acts of endearment. That's quite good cabaret.

It's easy to avoid campsites, though: in Scotland, you can

pitch your tent almost anywhere and enjoy beautiful, unspoiled countryside, as long as *you* don't spoil it. Or you can take a lightweight tent to the tops of the Munros, which is even better.

Unless you are one of those really determined characters, like Nervous Nigel, there are some hills you do over and over again just for the fun of it or because you can't face the ten-hour road trip to the other side of Inverness, stuck behind caravans or avoiding BMWs streaking straight at you like Scud missiles. *Take it easy.* Staying near home is better than wasting petrol on the off-chance that the weather might improve, and the pouring rain and low mist will disappear. The problem with some of the Munros is actually getting there; the huge journey to many of them make Scotland feel more like Texas than the northern part of a small island. At school, we were taught that Scotland is a small country with big cities; the reverse is actually true.

I often climb Ben Lawers. It's near Glasgow and the car park is halfway up the mountain, so it's a soft touch for its height. If you can avoid the wind, that is. For some reason, this hill seems to have more than a sumo on Guinness; sometimes it feels like you're walking in a jet-engine testing-tunnel. Alex and I started to wander up it one winter night shortly after midnight, which was not too bad considering we'd planned to arrive there around eight. The full moon was beaming down on us like a spotlight so we didn't need headtorches. Just as well, really, since Alex's had no battery anyway. For some reason, he thinks that when a battery runs out, if you leave it in the torch, it will recharge itself. We had decided to pitch a tent near the top for no particular reason other than to watch the cold stars and satellites gliding across space. As we walked off Beinn Ghlas, the Munro you plod over on the way to the summit of Ben Lawers, we were treated to a moonlit Brocken spectre.

You can see a Brocken spectre more or less any time you want, it's not a big deal. The way some of the hillwalking writers witter on, you would think it was an apparition from another dimension. All you have to do is stand with the sun shining down on you at an angle – duh, it's always at an angle unless you are on the equator – and have a misty gully below you. If you look down onto the mist, you will see a circular rainbow with your shadow projected into the middle of it. You can save yourself the walk and see one from the comfort of an aeroplane seat next time you fly to Amsterdam for a filthy weekend. Sun above on the left, cloud below on the right, plane in between. No problem. This, however, was a moonlit Brocken spectre. There we were, at 2 a.m. on a dark, Scottish mountain with our shadows shimmering on the mist inside a halo. Now *that* is atmospheric.

I was carrying a three-man tent, a full-bhuna winter sleeping bag, plus a big-ass self-inflating mat that was like a single bed and weighed almost as much. The Thermarest 'Fat Bastard' sleeping mat. The 'I Can't Believe It's Not a Bed' model. Or whatever it's called. The whole lot was heavy, but I don't mind hauling that kind of weight up a hill if I think I might get a decent night's sleep – although I know I won't. You either can or can't sleep well in tents. In one of his books, W.H. Murray, one of the best mountaineering writers, mentions that even on long expeditions in the Himalaya he couldn't get used to sleeping in tents and rarely managed more than a few hours' continuous shut-eye.

Alex, on the other hand, is a lucky bugger: he could sleep on a window ledge in a gale. We pitched the tent in the snow and lay with our heads poking out of the front, looking up towards the Milky Way and the galaxies of long, long ago, replaying that scene with Princess Leia, or simply recalling past lives on now deserted planets . . . that sort of thing. He asked if I had anything to drink other than water.

'Only Red Bull.'

'I'll have it.'

'You're going to drink a Red Bull at three in the morning just before you want to go to sleep?'

'Yeah.'

Fair enough. Red Bull probably has more caffeine than the

strongest espresso and definitely isn't sold as a nightcap; you don't want to drink an entire can just before bedding down for the night. Alex did. Then he belched, rolled over, farted twice and was purring happily in moments. Sometimes, he even laughs quietly in his sleep, which must be a good sign of something or other. It was a stormy night and the tent flapped like an old sail until about seven, when I finally dozed off for an hour or so. Alex slumbered like a baby on temazepam until ten. Didn't even get up in the night for a pee.

Ben An in the Trossachs is another great spot to pitch your tent. In winter, on a really cold night, it is superb; you feel you are in the middle of the universe.

If you pick up almost any hillwalking book or magazine, there's always someone chirping on about how gazing from the top of a mountain at all those distant stars gives them a sense of perspective, an insight into how insignificant they are. They are so damn predictable, so phoney – if they really felt that way, they wouldn't have the confidence to write about it. If I need reminding of what a small cog I am in the world, I stroll along the vast, glittering canyon of 57th Street in New York City. That really lets you realise what people can achieve without you. If anything, mountains can make you feel bigger, that you are alive and *part* of something vast, not separate from it.

The great thing about camping high is that you don't need to climb very high at all; small hills are just as good as Munros. I know a girl and her boyfriend, both of whom grew up in a bad part of Clydebank and are world-class climbers, although perhaps unsurprisingly not members of the Scottish Mountaineering Club. They like to make a night of it and regularly take wine and waccy-baccy up with them.

Glen Nevis is good, too. One night, Alex and I and his two children, Vicki and Justin, headed up there. I was trying to learn how to ski and Justin, who was only six at the time, was my instructor – I was fed up with Alex taking me straight onto black runs, which I clattered down like someone in the throes of a particularly spectacular seizure. *On you go, it's a dawdle . . . just think how easy you'll find the blue runs after you do this one.*

Jussie led me onto a nice, easy green slope, then patiently skied in front of me shouting, 'Turn . . . Turn . . . ' and I followed him until I got the knack, which made all the difference to how I felt about winter. I soon grew to love skiing so much that I forgot about the long, dark nights.

The night before, in way-below-zero temperatures, we'd camped in a very nice spot beside a 'No Camping' sign in the glen. As we queued next morning for tickets at Aonach Mor, a man from Bearsden pulled his thick, goose-down jacket further up around his ears and asked us if we'd driven up that morning.

'No,' smiled Jussie politely, 'we were camping.'

The man looked at him, then at me. Surely the boy was mistaken.

'You what . . .?'

'We were camping.' Jussie thought nothing of it. So what that it was nine below zero? He's been doing it since he was a baby. The man looked at Jussie and Vicki as if they had just travelled in by reindeer from the Russian tundra.

'Jesus Christ, you kids must be right hardy souls.'

In summer, it can be really nice stretched out in a tent on top of a hill, provided you check the forecast. One August night, I was restless. I had planned to meet a friend at Glencoe, but he'd called off. It was a hot, sunny night. I couldn't settle and decided to take off to Ben An with my little one-man tent, a lightweight thing that is really just a sheet of nylon stretched over a single metal pole. It was about eleven o'clock when I got to the top, then watched the last colours of the sunset before squeezing inside. It was really hot. Clammy as hell. Too hot to sleep. I lay on my mat reading, listening to Bob Harris on my little radio.

Bob is, of course, famous for *The Old Grey Whistle Test*. I'd always wanted to do that gig, but the BBC had banned the String Band for life. Mike and Robin, the founder members of the band, had done a show with Julie Felix and the producer had wanted her to do a duet with them. She chirped along on one of their songs and it sounded like a singalong at Butlins. I have seen the film of it and it is cringingly bad. They had taken the hump and buggered off. You don't walk off set and work for the Beeb again. Despite fans handing in a petition with 15,000 names, the ISB was never allowed to do any TV work in the UK.

'Whispering' Bob was coming over loud and clear in my little tent. It was getting hotter and hotter. I've spent a lot of time on the Gulf Coast of Florida (if you ever want to see spectacular lightning storms, go there in July), so I should have known what was happening, but this was Scotland and it just didn't occur to me. Then the rain started. Not the usual lightweight drizzly stuff you get here, but a downpour of biblical proportions. Bap, bap, bap, bap, bap, *bap, bap, bap*! Out of the dark sky, it hammered on to the thin nylon above me. I was perfectly dry inside, but it was getting even hotter and clammier.

Suddenly, there was a far-off flash of light. Then a crash of thunder. Oh, shit, of course, why did it not dawn on me? But it sounded far away. Then another flash of lightning. I counted the gap until the thunder . . . 20 seconds. And again . . . 15 seconds. I didn't breathe. Another much brighter flash of light. Only a five-second gap. *Bloody thing's coming right at me!*

It is funny how thoughts can last only a few microseconds, but cover a great deal of ground. As I waited to see what was about to happen next, I was terrifyingly aware that I was in a tiny tent on the pointed top of the highest thing around; all that was between me and the entire electrical power of the universe was a piece of thin nylon stretched across a quivering aluminium pole. I might as well have put up a lightning conductor and attached it to my head. I could picture the scene next morning: the tent burnt to cinders, my charred, dumb-ass body black and fried crispy in the ashes. I would have tried to run for it, but the rain was crashing down; I would have slipped and fallen down the mountain, which is dangerously steep, especially in the dark when it's wet. I felt a complete idiot. *This is what happens when you don't check the bloody forecast.*

Then the brightest, most intense burst of light, like the massive white stage spots The Who used to turn onto the audience, exploded all around – inside, outside the tent, it seemed to be everywhere – and at the same instant a deafening blast of thunder. The radio screamed a final choked static crackle and died. No more Bob. The next seconds seemed to last for ever. If the lightning hit the pole, the tent would explode in flames and cook me in a blaze of pyrotechnics. *Oh, shit, please pass over.* I waited, holding my breath. Don't know why, you just do.

Flash! Bang! But it was slightly further away. I breathed for the first time in two minutes and felt sweat pouring down my face. But the rain was still battering down – it was nearly five in the morning before it eased enough for me to risk going down the hill. I lay there all night, hair standing on end, eyes wide open, waiting for the next storm.

At least there were no sewage pipes overhead. Could have used one, though.

18

KNOCKING ON HEAVEN'S DOOR

Soft snow on hard ice

SOME THINGS IN LIFE ARE JUST DANGEROUS. IT'S THE WAY IT IS.

From as young as I can remember, everyone I knew was well aware that smoking was addictive, was bad for your health, made you stink and your teeth fall out, caused lung cancer and all sorts of other things. Cigarettes were called coffin nails. Various brands used to give gift certificates and the standing joke was that if you collected a million, you could redeem them for an iron lung. It was a mug's game. Everyone knew that, you only had to look at the old geezers slouching on any street corner with full-strength Woodbines dangling from their brown, nicotine-stained fingers, hawking their rattling lungs onto the pavement. Schoolkids could buy loose cigarettes from cafés – *a tipped single, please* – but if your father caught you with one, you would be safer running away to sea.

Teachers belted the hell out of kids caught smoking in school toilets; it was the worst possible offence at Hyndland School, other than jerking off in class. I remember a guy being caught for that during an English lesson – the miniskirts of the '60s were just too much for him. Poor bastard, he should have learned how to play guitar. The only reason I started on Embassy Regals was to make smoking hash easier; I wanted to be able to haul that smoke deep down without spluttering like a schoolgirl.

No one forced you to smoke. Even in those days, when advertisers could say pretty much anything they liked, you didn't see billboards claiming that 'Bensons Help You Breathe Better', 'Choose Capstan – the Coughless Cigarette' or 'Marathon Men Smoke Marlboro'. It had been a long time since I'd reached the point where I hated smoking and I'd finally managed to quit after sucking down two packs a day for almost twenty years – when you get through the stage where you feel like biting your face, you know you are getting somewhere. If I hadn't needed the lung-power for hillwalking, I wouldn't have managed it, or at least not until my heart twisted itself into a knot or I needed a leg lopped off at the knee. If I wanted to see the view from the top of a mountain, I needed all the oxygen I could swallow. I have boundless sympathy for anyone who is in the process of quitting and clawing themselves, but these people who claim compensation because they say they didn't realise it was harmful . . . I mean, come on. What did you *think* you were doing?

Other things in life are dangerous too. Like Scottish winter-climbing.

It is one of our hidden tourist attractions. Climbers, especially those gaunt gecko-types with blank, long-staring eyes, make pilgrimages to Scotland every year to have the living crap scared out of them on frozen rock faces and ice gullies all over the Highlands. It all began at the end of the nineteenth century when robust gents in tweed jackets and hobnailed boots were looking for an alternative to the French Alps, there being no easyJet flights at the time. They were brave characters, climbing to giddy heights by cutting steps in the snow-ice up the terrifyingly steep, cold north faces on many of the Munros. Ever since, mountaineers from all over the world dream of making at least one trip to Scotland to climb in the birthplace of the sport.

Scotland is a unique winter-climbing venue: Scottish mountains have hundreds of climbs that are the equal of many routes in the Alps in terms of technical difficulty, but at a much lower altitude. They are much easier to reach, so it is possible for even the most skilful climbers to find as hard a route as they could possibly want, get themselves into all sorts of trouble, and still be down in time for a beer and bullshit session with other maniacs in front of a roaring pub fire. In the Alps, it is often necessary to take a cable car or slowly hike halfway up the mountain and sleep in one of the packed communal huts among other nervously tossing-and-turning climbers, hopelessly trying to ignore the cacophony of farting and snoring before everyone charges out to make a 2 a.m. start. You have to do this to avoid the rockfalls that occur in the Alps when the afternoon sun hits the slopes and melts the ice. In Scotland, you can have a good fry-up and not leave your car until seven o'clock. Or even later, if you're a bit mental.

Then there is the sheer unpredictability of the climbs. Owing to often rapidly changing weather, the routes are rarely the same two days in a row. On Saturday, they might be in what climbers call 'good condition', chock-full with a mixture of beautifully solid honeycombed ice and frozen snow; on Sunday, after a slight temperature change, they can be a horror story of collapsing powder avalanches or wet slush. Even worse, the rock might be coated with a razor-thin covering of lethal ice – verglas – too thin to sink the point of an axe into, but ferociously slippy – it's like trying to climb a plate-glass window. There are so many variable factors in Scotland, sometimes – often – you can get a mixture of great and horrendous conditions on the same climb on the same day. The weather can turn in an instant from crisp and sunny to an arctic blizzard. When this happens, climbers can soon find themselves in a battle to stay alive – these dramas are called 'epics'. They will do anything they can to escape to safety; if there is nothing else available, they'll even sink their ice axes into frozen turf, trusting it to hold their weight. Hell, they'll even pray. But experienced winter-climbers all say the same thing; when it is good, it is the best in the world.

It is dangerous. I sometimes wonder if it will be made illegal, if legislators in Brussels will use health-and-safety laws to impose impossible restrictions on climbing instructors so they won't be able to get insurance, making them easy meat for lawyers if anything goes wrong. That doesn't mean that no one will go winter-climbing, simply that no qualified guides will be able to teach it, which will make it even more dangerous. It will just take one claim and the wrong judge – who would have thought 30 years ago that tobacco companies could be sued?

The SMC publish superb little guidebooks, the winter-climbers' equivalent of *The Munros*, which show the routes of established climbs, all graded according to difficulty. Future historians will be amazed at what we did in our winter holidays. One of these books, called, perhaps a tad predictably, *Scottish Winter Climbs*, has some of the most absorbing photographs you will ever see anywhere. Buy it just to look at the pictures when you are tucked up cosy in bed on a stormy winter night. Those are real climbers in there, clinging like limpets to impossibly steep ice cliffs, often in hideous weather, one small slip away from death. Some of the photographs look like paintings, they are so dramatic, yet the book is modest and restrained, simply outlining the routes. It's even designed to fit in a climber's pocket for easy reference whilst battling up some desperate ice face or other. It makes fascinating reading.

If the Highlands has a spell of cold temperatures that freeze the ground nice and hard, then a good dump of snow falls, followed by thaw–freeze cycles (when the snow starts to melt during the day, then freezes hard overnight), you get perfect conditions for winter-climbing. When a climb is in 'good condition' and you swing your axe into the ice, it will bite reassuringly first time, then up you go. A simple kick with the points of your crampons will pierce the thick, frozen surface and, if you were not quite right in the head, you could stand there all day, hundreds of feet up a cliff face or high in a narrow gully, with a manic grin on your face, and you'd be quite secure.

When snow- and ice-climbs are in this condition, they are said to be 'in good nick'. Climbers jab stubby fingers onto their mobile phones, calling their mates, enthusiastically telling them such and such a route is 'in' – once they've grabbed it themselves, of course. Emails and texts fly all over the place, climbers' websites buzz with excitement.

While the vast majority of the population are shovelling snow out of their driveways, pulling their duvets over their heads or bitching about the freezing temperatures bursting their pipes, an entire alt-world of excitement is building all over the country. The colder it gets, the better. You can meet lean, hardcore climbers flying into Scotland from places like Canada, America and France, where you really would have thought there was more than enough ice to keep them busy. Winter-climbing in the breathtaking beauty of the Scottish Highlands can be that good.

As winter deepens, climbers patiently wait for these thaw–freeze cycles, watching the skies, charts, thermometers, Met Office forecasts and websites, quietly sharpening their axes, a bit like Robert Shaw in *Jaws*. Gradually, gullies become solid staircases of crusty, frozen snow; during a really cold winter even waterfalls freeze, although usually only for a few days. When that happens, mad men and women from all over Britain race through the night to try to be first on the best climbs, so highly prized are good winter-climbing conditions. You would be amazed how busy the A82 is at four o'clock in the morning. If you were sitting at the top of any of the more popular cliffs on Ben Nevis, Creag Meagaidh, the 'Gorms or Glen Coe in the middle of the night, freezing your ass off, you would see pinpoints of light deep down below, lines of little bobbing headtorches racing uphill, climbers elbowing each other out of the way to get to the start of the best routes.

Some of them take the whole thing very seriously and jostle irritably in the pre-dawn darkness to get to a climb first, watching other climbers and trying to assess them. The reason is that while all climbers deny that they would ever chop up a route (hack at it with their ice axes), they are convinced that everyone else will be amateurs who will do exactly that and cut the ice to pieces, destroying it. When you are climbing vertical snow and ice, you have to feel sure that your axe is embedded enough that you can pull up on it. Another concern is that if a nervous climber is above, he may flail and chop at the snow/ice and bring down chunks of it onto whoever is below. This can be more than a mild annoyance – I know a climber who lost an eye due to an earthbound splinter of ice. A big enough piece can decapitate you.

The alternative to starting early is starting late when most other climbers are finishing, or 'topping out' as it's called. Very few people do this because of the risk of becoming stuck on the route, frightened and freezing your nuts off all night, which in Scotland in January is a long night indeed . . . anything up to 17 cold, lonesome hours. You can't just blunder about in the dark hoping you will find an easy way off – unless you are certain you know an escape route, you are safer to sit it out until daylight, even if you shiver all night. This, in the curious climbers' language that has developed, is called being 'benighted'.

I know I am digressing, but there is an interesting tendency among outdoor writers to use these obscure words. Benighted, bejewelled, atop, ice-girt and, one of the most common, crag-girt, which simply means there are a lot of cliffs, so watch where you're going. This habit is a sort of written equivalent of those Scottish folk singers who stick a finger in one ear then warble out songs about long-gone fishermen in a strange nasal accent you never hear anywhere else. Or the computer programmers who yatter on about populating databases, cascading information, illegal operations, mandatory fields and all the rest. It's all very entertaining.

But back to the point. There is not much daylight in Scotland in January, especially at the beginning of the month. If the 'So You Want to Commit Suicide Society' ever holds a convention, it will be in Scotland in late December or early January, when the sun barely blinks in the morning and then starts to slink down shortly after noon, like a scolded dog. The light is pale and weak, and if it is overcast, you'd better have a good supply of Prozac or St John's wort. It's de-fucking-pressing.

So, what better way to instil a new appreciation of life than to scare yourself shitless by whimpering your way up a Scottish winter-climb? For my first attempt, I really should have done something much easier, but Alex grinned and said the North Buttress on the Bookle would be ideal; a dawdle, in fact. If you are daft enough to attempt to climb this cold, brooding wall of icy rock in January and you want to avoid getting stuck all night on it, you should start nice and early.

I'm not very good at that. I don't like having to get up when it's still dark. I always think I haven't set the clock properly and that my back-up, my mobile phone, will run out of power in the middle of the night. If I have get up before dawn to catch a plane, for example, it's impossible to sleep. Every time I nod off, I start dreaming that I have missed the flight and jerk awake. I have been told it's like sleeping with someone who's receiving electro-convulsive therapy.

On the other hand, if I don't *have* to get up early, then it's no problem, I don't need an alarm clock. I always sleep with the window open, so the local milk boys often wake me. It is very pleasant to hear the birds sing, the gentle purr of the milk float, the light jingle-jangle of bottles, the young lad quietly whistling a cheerful tune as he softly places three pints at my door. Occasionally, you even catch a snippet of their morning banter as they call to each other from opposite sides of the road.

'Haw, Jakey, how'd you get on wi' that bird last night?'

'Aye, brilliant, wee man. Ah shagged the arse off her.'

Summer or winter, Alex always starts late. He likes to take his time; he doesn't do anything in a hurry. It is part of his charm. I have shared many hotel rooms with him on loads of European climbing and skiing trips, and it is actually quite delightful to see how much pleasure he derives from luxuriating in the simple pleasures of life. Each day starts with an unvarying routine. He enters the bathroom before breakfast with a thick magazine rolled up under his arm and a look of anticipation. Twenty minutes later, you hear vigorous flushing segueing into the sound of the shower pouring forth a steaming Niagara of hot water. Thus, the first 45 minutes of the day gently passes. Then breakfast, each glass of orange juice, bowl of cereal, croissant with boiled egg, hot buttered toast with honey and cup of tea slowly savoured. Replete, a stretch, a grin and another visit to the bathroom for a shave followed by a second sit down to round up any stragglers.

When you have arranged to meet Alex, don't set your alarm – arrange for him to pick you up and tell him to call you when he is leaving his house. You will have plenty of time to shower, breakfast, go to the supermarket and perhaps take care of some odd jobs around the house before he finally appears at your door. The latest he has been is five hours. When a load of us turned up at his restaurant of choice to join him for his birthday dinner, we had finished the melon and were halfway though the minestrone by the time he appeared. Why worry?

Originally, three of us had planned to go on the trip, but the other guy had called off. Or, in fact, his wife had called off for him, she'd heard all about Alex . . . Just the two of us then.

I was feeling grim. I'd been working all week despite having a heavy cold – you have to keep the business coming in – but I didn't want to let Alex down, so I dozed all the way to Glencoe in his old Land-Rover – a scrapyard on wheels, that thing, rattling and bouncing all the way up the A82. I reckoned I would feel better by the time I had swallowed a couple of cups of strong coffee at the Kings House Hotel – there is no chance of either of us doing anything without our usual jolt of caffeine first.

So we finally found ourselves, well after eleven o'clock, parking in the snow near the foot of the climbers' path up the Bookle. More sensible climbers had already reached the top of the mountain and were coiling their ropes, getting ready to walk back down to a celebratory drink. I was dubious about the whole escapade, mainly because my cold felt like it was taking on the grip of flu. I knew I shouldn't have been anywhere but in front of a fire that day with a hot lemon drink, but what the hell. I'd read somewhere that winter-climbing was good for getting rid of colds; I'd shake it off.

The first thing you have to get used to with Scottish winter-climbing is the sheer bloody weight you have to carry: ropes, crampons, ice axes, all the fiddly bits of metallic gear you need and warm clothes for when you are shivering on a ledge belaying your partner, waiting for them to get up to the next stance. All these things are heavy. As you walk up to the foot of the climb, you sweat like an over-the-hill heavyweight boxer, no matter how cold it is.

It was a steep trudge of almost two hours up through hard-packed snow to reach the foot of the North Buttress and, by then, I felt like someone waiting in a queue at an infectious-diseases unit. I realised it might not be the best day for this; I'd done enough winter hillwalking to know how tiring it is slogging through snow. Then I lifted my head and looked at what Alex was expecting me to climb. *He's fucking insane.* It was so bloody steep, it disappeared into the sky.

The North Buttress is a huge, evil face of steep and, in parts, crumbly black rock split by vertical cracks. These had the required snow and ice frozen into them, and it was up this that Alex was now climbing while I belayed him from below, wondering, between sneezes, why I had agreed to this. Alex is very persuasive. He made it look simple: swinging his axe into the ice, *thunk*, swinging the other one, *thunk*; pulling his foot back and kicking with his crampon; stepping up and kicking in the other one. He's been doing this every winter for over 25 years; his first winter-climbs were with old wooden-handled ice axes and his mother's washing line. The only reason it hadn't broken was because he hadn't fallen. I watched him with admiration – he was confident and competent, and completely relaxed.

He shot up quickly and, it seemed to me, very dangerously, the rope snaking behind him. He didn't bother trying to put in any equipment to protect him if he fell, since there really was nowhere to put it; any little cracks were blocked with hard ice. When the rope was near its full length, he called down to me that he was safe on a ledge and I should start climbing whenever I was ready. I gulped. Looked straight up. Swallowed hard again.

What the hell have I let myself in for this time?

I had borrowed climbing crampons and little curved axes that were not exactly new or sharp, but thankfully felt quite secure as I quickly whacked and kicked up to where Alex was balanced. I climbed fast out of sheer terror. When you are relying on rusty ice-axe points to grip brittle ice, you enter a new level of apprehension. Your mouth dries and you chop your way up the climb as fast as you can in case you seize up altogether. You wonder what the bloody hell a man your age is playing at. You wish you'd listened to your wife. Although the air is freezing, sweat pours down your face and mists up your specs. I'd always thought roller-coaster rides were frightening, but they are over in a few minutes; a winter-climb like this lasts hours and each moment can be terrifying.

I was just starting to get used to it and relax a little when I realised it was getting dark. I knew that I could walk down in the dark from the top of the Bookle if I could get there, but on the steep climb on which we were precariously poised, like a couple of flies on a wet flagpole, I had no way of knowing how far we had to go to reach it. I looked up and all I could see was more rock and ice disappearing darkly into the sky. Alex climbed up to another ledge and called down. I swung my axes hand over hand, again and again, kicked my crampons into the frozen surface, balanced on the edges of rocks poking through the ice and, a feverish sweat pouring off me, at last joined him at the next precarious stance he'd hacked into the snow. My legs were quivering. We were very high above Glen Coe; when I looked down between my knees I could see the road far below my feet. Little trails of car headlights threaded their way along in the dark like a far-off procession, sensible people heading home for a hot bath, perhaps even a pizza. Soon, all remaining light was gone. It was cold, black and silent.

'Eh . . . how far have we got to go, Alex?'

'Not far now, it's all over in a minute.'

We climbed on, hacking, balancing, edging and scraping up the dark icy cliff and reached the top of a pinnacle of rock jutting into the air. There was a gap between it and the snow-covered rock face, which fell back and continued up into the starless sky. Alex looked at it carefully. I looked at him. *What now?*

'Sorry to keep harping on, Alex, but how near are we to the end?'

'Oh . . . it'll be up here. Not far.'

My bones were aching. I was definitely coming down with flu. This was the last place I felt like being right now and I began to feel irritable.

'Alex, I thought you knew this route? When did you do it last?'

'I haven't.'

'What?'

'I haven't, it's the first time I've climbed it.'

'For fuck's sake! So you don't know what's up ahead?'

'More snow and ice.'

'Jesus Christ, you're kidding! We're up here, can't see a fucking thing and you don't know where we are?'

'Behave yourself.' He grinned, not in the least tense. 'Of course I know where we are. We're on the Bookle. We're climbing the North Buttress. In the dark. Enjoy the atmosphere. We're not far away now. Just relax, you're doing fine.'

He paused and pointed his headtorch from the top of the pinnacle over to the cliff face. The dim yellow beam barely reached it. *When will he learn to change his batteries?* On the other side of the gap was a horribly steep ramp, thick with ice and snow. He peered far up it, then turned to me.

'Eh . . . this isn't a recognised climbing technique, but it will save time. Watch me a minute. Give me out a bit of rope.'

He held his axes in the air in front of him and jumped from the pinnacle into the darkness straight at the angled ice face. *What the fuck . . .?*

Despite the sweat pouring down my face, I shivered and gripped the climbing rope in case he shot down the frozen ramp and off the cliff beneath. The points of his axes bit solidly and he kicked in his crampons.

'Ya beauty! It's brilliant! I'll go on up a bit, then you follow me. You'll love it.'

I waited until he called down to me.

'OK, come on, go for it.'

I glanced down. Everything below me was black; a terrible drop underneath. I knew what happened to climbers who fell from places like this. In the movies, it was a peaceful image of someone having met their end doing something they loved; a still body, a last smile of contentment. The reality is different. To fall from this height meant your body would be smashed and ripped to pieces on every piece of rock it battered against on the way down. The police wouldn't need a stretcher, just a couple of polythene bags for the bits that had been you. A pal had once retrieved a climber's helmet that still had half the guy's head inside it.

I began to shake, terrified. *He wants me to fucking jump. In the dark above a 1,000-ft drop, for fuck's sake. He wants me to fucking jump.* I felt him tug the rope. There was nothing else for it; it was impossible to climb back down. I pointed my headtorch at the cliff and leapt off the pinnacle into the cold air at the frozen snow face and whacked in my axes. Instinctively, I kicked into the ice, biting in the points of my crampons and frantically chopped up to Alex, swinging and kicking, my freezing breath pumping out mist, sweat pouring down my face.

'There you go!' He was taking in the rope, completely relaxed. 'That's the main climbing over. Just got to get up to the top now.'

I looked up. The angle had eased, but above us the frozen snow was banked out. It looked overhanging. I peered into the white arc of my headtorch. *Shit, it is overhanging. What the hell do we do now?*

He nodded ahead. 'We just have to get above that, then it's a straight walk up.'

There was a boulder sticking out of the snow and I threw a sling round it, clipped myself to it then prepared to belay Alex as he climbed up to the banked-out cornice. He was loving every minute of this, totally in his element. I was miserable. I watched him climb across and round a corner, then out of sight. I felt totally alone. It was completely dark, moonless, with black clouds racing high above, blocking out any starlight. *Never again.* I realised that if he fell, the only thing holding me to this boulder was one sling. If he slipped, he would go flying past. I would be whipped off the buttress and we would become a trail of shattered bone and flesh all over the dark cliff below us. *Great, just bloody great.*

I fed the last few feet of rope out to him and it went tight. He hadn't called to me, so it could only mean that he'd reached the full length and hadn't found somewhere safe to stop. He was still climbing, pulling on the rope. *What the fuck am I supposed to do now?* I had to follow or the taut rope would stop him going any further and might pull him from the cliff face. Then we'd die. I whipped the sling off the boulder – it came loose in my hands far too easily. I was shaking, partly through fear, partly through the heavy cold that was chilling me. Neither of us was belayed now; one slip would be disaster. Adrenalin and fear surged through me. I would rather have been anywhere else than here.

Shit, this is steep. I climbed up, following the slack rope, then, at last, it tightened; he had stopped and found somewhere to belay. I kept climbing, trying not to panic, slowing my breathing, and finally reached Alex. He was calmly gathering in the rope, standing on a small ledge he'd hacked in the snow, oblivious to the huge drop beneath us; his shoulder leaning against the steep slope, cigar in his mouth, the red tip glowing in the darkness.

'We're nearly there. Just a tad more climbing, then a straightforward walk up. You're doing great.'

'Eh, Alex, what are you belayed into?' He blew out a stream of smoke and nodded towards his axes. They were both buried deep in the snow with a sling round them that he was clipped into with a karabiner.

'Oh, shit. You're kidding! Is that all that would stop us if we fell?'

'We're not going to fall.' He grinned and patted my arm. 'Just relax. Right, push in your axes as far as they will go.'

He watched as I shoved them into the snow, which seemed just firm enough to take them. He checked that I was clipped to the axes then pulled his; they popped out without the slightest effort, not solid at all. I clipped the belay plate to the sling, fed the rope through it and held it with my ice-crusted gloves. *What bloody good will this be if he falls?*

'Right, I'm going up this bit, then it's all over.'

He stepped to the side and then methodically swung each axe in turn above his head, driving the points into the brittle frozen snow, which was banked so far out that it hung ominously over him in the darkness like a guillotine. The top of the mountain was somewhere up there, but we couldn't see it. He clambered and kicked up and over the bulge, and disappeared again. I fed out the rope and glanced at my axes. The bloody things had pulled right out. I had been right, the snow was too soft to grip them and, anyway, because Alex was straight above, the rope was yanking them out as he climbed. He was completely out of sight. *A tad more climbing? This is what he calls a tad more fucking climbing.* I felt a wave of utter fear grip me.

In climbing, there are several stages of terror. Roughly speaking, they start with whinging (*this is too difficult*). Then anger (*what the fuck are we doing up here?*) followed by begging (*can we please just get off this?*), trembling (*can't go any further, I'm stuck*), panic (*I'm going to fall . . . we're going to die*) and finally paralysis.

Climbers call the state of paralysis being 'gripped'. It is a word rarely used outside climbing circles. Anyone who has been in a dangerous situation on a climb knows the feeling of being gripped. The word terror does not begin to cover it. Unfortunate victims cannot move, every muscle seizes and they become unable to climb out of the situation, whilst hideously aware of all the reasons they shouldn't have attempted the climb in the first place. It is not a nice feeling. It is the body's response to the prospect of imminent death.

Experienced climbers learn to recognise the feeling of becoming gripped and will act quickly to prevent it – it's generally thought they have no fear of heights, but everyone has. Only those who belong in a long-stay ward with large daffodils painted on the wall would enjoy feeling that they are about to plummet to their death. Normally, a climber will find something he can do – anything – to keep him moving or at least make him feel he is in control. It might be something as simple as putting another piece of gear into a crack, tidying up coils of rope or checking the belay to which he is clipped. Maybe just having a drink of water or even enjoying a long, satisfying fart. The last thing he wants is to feel totally out of control because, of course, at that point, paralysis definitely will set in. When that happens, he ain't going anywhere. Except, perhaps, very swiftly to the ground and the nearest mortuary.

It is very, very easy to get gripped when you are oh so tenuously balanced on the tiny points of little metal axes and crampons in total darkness on a vertical sheet of frozen snow and brittle ice; the hard, cold, rocky ground is a long, long way below your fluttering arse and you know with utter certainty that if you do not *get a fucking grip of yourself right fucking now, you stupid bastard*, you will fall and die. And when you arrive at that frame of mind, the expression 'to be wise after the event' takes on a whole new sickening lucidity.

The overhanging snow face Alex had disappeared up looked certain to collapse and I knew if – when – that happened, absolutely nothing could stop us crashing down that awful drop below. At moments like that, you feel overwhelming regret – *why was I naive enough to be talked into this?* You remember pleasant hillwalking, strolling up Munros in the sunshine, and swear if you ever get out of this alive, you will never, ever put yourself in this position again. I suddenly thought of my sons and how stupid I was – one slip and I would never see them again. I pictured a sunny, palm-tree-lined beach in Florida and how I would give anything to stroll along it with them, watching them splash in the gentle, warm Gulf Coast waves. Anything instead of freezing and shaking here. A piece of classical music, Albinoni's *Adagio*, kept swirling round my head. I pushed my face into the frozen snow straight in front of me and felt a deathly chill on my forehead. I shivered. I was becoming totally gripped. I had to do something quick or I'd had it. *Get your fucking head up!*

Alex's voice drifted down from a long way above. 'Right. I'm safe here . . . come on.'

As soon as I heard his voice, I hit the huge overhanging bulge and charged up it. *Do it! Fucking just get on with it!* There was no time to think, no carefully placed axes; it was self-preserving, almost panic-stricken climbing. I reckoned the hard, banked-out snow was too unstable to allow me more than one whack with my axes on each move before it would collapse. *There's no time to fart about.* All I could think was, get on with it, *get yourself out of this nightmare.*

Somehow, I managed to pull my chest above the edge, kicking and swinging my legs up over the overhang, and at last the cliff fell back to an easier ramp, but it was completely dark. I couldn't see Alex anywhere.

'Hey, Alex, where the hell are you?'

Suddenly I could see the dim yellow glow of his headtorch about 40 ft above me.

'See this headtorch, Graham? I'm underneath it.'

Yeah, very funny. I grinned and climbed the slope up to him. Another little ledge hacked out of the snow. He was smiling; a happy man.

'Brilliant, eh?' He nodded over his shoulder. 'It's an easy climb the rest of the way to the top. A canter. Did you enjoy that?'

I looked at him through the hot sweat stinging my eyes and felt a rush of relief. The top of the Bookle was still about 300 ft higher. We were not safe yet. We needed to get up and over to the other side before we could make our way down. The snow sloped upwards at an angle of about 40 degrees, the perfect angle for avalanches. It was icy and dark. I'd had enough of being afraid: if we were going to fall, we were going to fall. *If we're going to fucking die, we're going to fucking die.* A rage exploded in my head. *Fuck this.*

'Right, I'm going first, Alex. Let's get the fuck out of here!'

I charged on up the slope, carefully but quickly placing each spiked boot, my axes ready just in case. I could feel my heart pounding and sweat pouring down my face and back, even in the subzero temperature. One slip . . . it would be horrific: crashing back down the slope, trying to stop with the axes, accelerating, too fast, knowing that a 1,000-ft sheer drop was hurtling up to meet you.

At last, I realised I was at the top and I stepped up the last few feet to the cairn of rocks piled at the summit. Immediately, the wind howled at us from the unsheltered side of the mountain; we could only see a short distance, our headtorches unable to penetrate far into the blackness. But now all we had to do was walk down the other side; 3,000 ft or so, a couple of hours, and we would be safe. *We're gonna be all right, we're gonna be all fucking right.* I felt a glow of relief, my rigid muscles relaxed and slackened. *Thank God that's over.* I swore that I would never, ever ice-climb again. Never. *Never again.*

The strange thing is that I very quickly forgot how terrifying these things are and soon found myself longing to be back, feeling the axes bite into frozen snow. I can't explain it because virtually every winter-climb I've done since had at least a few moments of utter terror. Rocks come crashing down just missing you; mini-avalanches of powdery snow pour over you; ice cracks apart like a breaking dinner plate and your axe flies out, swinging you round against the face as you desperately try to keep balanced; a crampon springs off on some horribly steep section; ledges collapse beneath you; sudden blizzards hammer into you, dark winds howling like elemental spirits. Once more, you swear that you will never go near ice again, but three days later you have forgotten the fear and you are gazing out of your office window at a clear blue winter sky, knowing what is waiting for you up north. It's crazy.

Winter-climbing is risky but, like cigarettes, you get hooked. I don't know why it is so addictive. It just is. It shouldn't be.

It's not as dangerous as smoking, though. Honest.

19

SYMPATHY FOR THE DEVIL

Fear

FEAR. IT'S A SCARY THING.

When you get into the habit of climbing, you soon realise that at some point in the day, you may shit yourself. Once you accept that, you are halfway to controlling it. Fear is unavoidable. In fact, I am very wary of climbing with anyone who doesn't occasionally get scared – they are usually dangerous bastards.

I reckon there are three sources of fear: things that everyone can see, things that only you can see, and things that no one can see. Most people regard climbing as frightening and, as I was well aware, it can be, although once you become used to being up there, learn about keeping your balance on steep rock and gain confidence, it becomes more exhilarating than terrifying. It is like stepping onto a stage in front of 25,000 people – if you know exactly what you are going to play, you can harness the adrenalin that nerves produce and channel it into your playing.

When you run a business, there's plenty to worry about, you

never learn to completely relax; you have to get used to sleepless nights or book yourself into the Jolly Gibberer Sanatorium while you are still able to feed yourself. The most successful people I know worry the most: they are always thinking about work. If they stop caring about what is happening, their businesses might start falling apart. The sort of people who build companies are usually not contented folk – if they were, they would have settled down in a 9-to-5 job soon after leaving school and spend their weekends decorating.

Worse are the demons that haunt a man that only he can see, until he tries to drown them with *the drink*, or with drugs . . . or by climbing routes alone without a rope or any kind of protection against a fall. This is known as soloing. Perhaps it works because the intense concentration required sucks up every spark of mental energy, positive and negative, until, at the end, only stillness remains. It is bloody stupid and I never tell my family when I've been doing it, but sometimes . . .

I know I keep taking cheap shots at climbing books – it is just that I find the writers painfully shallow and clichéd as they stride manfully among the bloody bog myrtle, birdsong and flowers, not a care in the world. Well, yippee. A rare exception is an article I read in an American magazine that was written by a big-wall climber called Travis Boyette. He is a crack-cocaine addict and makes no excuses.

He managed to quit when he discovered he could burn off the 'longing' by climbing alone on the fearsome rock faces of Yosemite. Eventually, he was able to calm his mind and found a good woman, married, got a steady job and became an accepted member of the quiet rural town in which they settled. Whenever his demons were threatening to overwhelm him like a returning hurricane, he would quietly make his way to the towering sandstone cliffs and climb solo for as long as it took. Deep inside was the memory that crack-cocaine could release him too, instantly, and it was always waiting. It knew they would meet again sooner or later; it was just a question of time. He couldn't climb for ever.

When he shook hands with his old friend again, he only intended it to be once, just to prove to himself he had beaten it. A month later, he had lost everything it had taken him so long to work for, and his wife left, sobbing, knowing she could never compete with crack. Soon after, he was arrested in possession and when he wrote his article, he had become prisoner T-40383, sitting in a stifling, cramped cell in California with another year to serve of his sentence, watching his back, quietly dreaming of the day he would find his way back to the valley to climb again.

Then there are things that no one can see.

One winter night, I was driving up to the Cluanie Inn at Glen Shiel. It was freezing, great forecast, cloudless all the way from Holland to Cape Cod. I was in a good mood, was heading to meet the Lecturer next day for some plodding through the snow on the long ridge that hangs high above the road through the glen. As I drove out of Fort William and up through Invergarry, I kept looking up at the stars, thousands of them glittering in the inky sky. I even drove with my lights off for short spells – I had to get a better look.

I stopped the car beside the road above Loch Loyne, switched off the engine and got out, leaned against the front and gazed up. It was beautiful: the clear, endlessly deep, black starry sky you can only see when you are in the Highlands, miles from any town. It was absolutely silent, a hush you could almost feel. Then, suddenly, it was on me, a feeling of utter malevolence, of hatred beyond depth or breadth or reason. Everywhere. It seemed to fill every inch of the frozen air surrounding me. I have never been so afraid.

It was as if I had entered the space of something evil; a single, overwhelming thought rushed at me so clearly it gripped me completely. *Leave, leave here now.* The words were full of contempt. I had no business being there. One word came to me, I don't know why or from where, but it was suddenly in my head, the only word I could think of: Pan, as in *everywhere*. It felt as though all the evil in the world was gathered in that

149

suddenly awful place. I leapt back into the car and slammed the door, breathing hard. After a few moments, the windscreen had misted up and I opened the window and looked out into the still night air, trying to calm down, telling myself this was ludicrous. Instantly, I felt a horrible wave of hate washing over me, drowning me in panic. My one thought: get away from here, now.

My hands trembled and I could feel my heart pumping as I twisted the key in the ignition and raced off. Half an hour later, I reached the Cluanie Inn and stepped out the car. I walked a little way from the car park, then a little further, away from the light of the small hotel. I was perfectly calm, looking up at the same stars, which now seemed to have had a veil removed from them: they were beautiful again. For a long time, I stood alone in the darkness. *What the hell was that all about?*

Eventually, I forgot about it, until a couple of years later when I was glancing through a magazine in one of Alex's shops. It was a warm midsummer's day, but a sudden chill ran through me. In one of the articles, there was a quotation from a book by the Scottish writer John Buchan in which he describes walking down through woods and meadows on a June morning in 1910, after climbing in the Alps.

> I noticed that my companion had fallen silent, and . . . was amazed to see that his face was dead-white, that sweat stood in beads on his forehead, and that his eyes were staring ahead as if he was in an agony of fear, as if terror were all around him . . . Suddenly he began to run, and I ran too, some power not myself constraining me. Terror had seized me also, but I did not know what I dreaded . . .

Buchan goes on to describe:

> . . . moments when one feels a kind of personal malevolence, the sense of a hostile will which almost

takes bodily form and which sets the nerves fluttering . . .
In such moments one sees, or at any rate feels, what the
ancients meant by Pan.

I read the article again, scarcely breathing. It was identical to
my experience; an invisible fear that was so powerful it gripped
me completely, a terror that was impossible to conquer. Even
the same word: Pan. What the hell was it?

In all the mountain ranges of the world, there seems to be a
local tradition of fear, which is strange bearing in mind the
peaceful beauty of the surroundings. Where there is fear, there
is religion, and many mountains are regarded as the dwelling
places of gods, some benevolent, some evil. In an article in *The
Times* (the London one) in 2003, the writer and mountaineer Ed
Douglas wrote: 'The Tibetan myths about mountains are
populated with wrathful deities, ghosts or terrible creatures
such as the Yeti. They are warnings to stay away.' He went on
to discuss Everest, or Chomolungma, as the locals call it:

> The goddess said to inhabit the slopes of Chomolungma
> is Miyolangsangma . . . one of a group of wrathful deities
> . . . Sherpas on Everest go out of their way to keep on her
> good side; offensive smells, such as roasting meat or
> burning garbage, rubbish and morally questionable
> behaviour, can provoke her wrath. Before every
> expedition they will hold a puja, building a *lhap-so*,
> which is a kind of altar, and stringing up lines of prayer
> flags to bring good luck.

A pal who has climbed Everest told me there was a bit of bother
one night at base camp when a guide and his American client
decided to take their climbing partnership one step further. For
some reason, as many touring rock bands discover with joy,
American girls often make a great deal of noise at exactly the
right moments, and the wailing, moaning and gasps of carnal
ecstasy from their tent caused an angry response from the

Sherpas, who were not amused. They coitally interrupted the pair without any ceremony.

As far as I know, Ben Macdui in the Cairngorms is the only Scottish mountain that has a record of some sort of ominous presence. In 1925, Professor Norman Collie stood up at an Annual General Meeting of the Cairngorm Climbing Club and described the sense of dread that seized him as he walked off the mountain and heard what sounded like huge footsteps following him. He told the audience that he raced off in terror 'like a frightened kitten'.

Collie was the first professor of organic chemistry at the University of London, a man 'sardonic and dry as dust in manner, he did not suffer fools gladly'. He was one of the first great international mountaineers, a practical man who had calmly climbed some of the most dangerous places in the Alps, the Himalaya and the Rockies, a man used to being alone for long periods in the most inhospitable places and not given to whimsical flights of fantasy. In those days, ridicule was the worst thing that could happen to a professional person like Collie and he must have realised the risk he was taking speaking about the incident; he had kept it a secret for over a quarter of a century.

Like thousands of other hillwalkers, I have hiked up Ben Macdui alone, but have never experienced anything other than relief on finally reaching the top, at which point I've gulped down a Red Bull and wondered how long it will take me to walk the long miles back to the car. The vast majority of people who do it probably experience something similar. Not all of them, though. There are other reports of climbers feeling terror on or very near Ben Macdui, sometimes accompanied by the sound or sight of a huge, ghostly figure, like an abominable snowman or Bigfoot. Sometimes it is simply an unknown, unseen fear; a presence of hatred overwhelming them.

If it was simply my imagination, I don't know why I'd never felt it when I was sleeping alone in a little tent at the tops of mountains, or wandering alone across the gloomy summit ridge of Ben Nevis in thick mist at one o'clock in the morning, or so many other times when I was sitting at the top of a hill somewhere in the dead of night staring at the stars. Out of hundreds of trips into the hills, this was the only time it has ever happened to me. And thank God for that.

A couple of years later, I stopped at the same spot and it was simply a beautiful place to be again. It felt completely different, as though it had been reprieved, as though something had now left. I had planned to work the weekend, but when I saw the forecast – high pressure everywhere – I knew Saturday would be great and so I shot off up north to Beinn Sgritheall, a jagged lone Munro overlooking Loch Hourn. When you live in the city and you seek out these remote hills, it often feels like you are visiting another country. Doubtless the local residents have the same daily hassles that trouble the rest of us, like being preoccupied simply trying to find a decent job, but their little villages look so tranquil. How could anyone feel the presence of evil in such beauty?

Evidently, some people do. A famous mountaineer, Aleister Crowley, bought Boleskin House, overlooking Loch Ness, where he spent frenzied years trying to conjure up various devils. Nearby residents really could complain about neighbours from hell. Naming himself 'the Great Beast 666', he formed a cult called Thelema, with the simple rule: 'Do what thou wilt shall be the whole of the law.' Handy that, covers pretty much everything. Since drug-taking and ritualistic sex orgies were part of a normal Saturday night for his devotees, the house saw some pretty wild parties. Years later, Jimmy Page, who thought Crowley was a 'misunderstood genius', bought the house and, among other things, used it to film some bizarre sequences for a movie.

It is odd that the Highlands should have a long folklore of witches, fairies, goblins, vampires and evil spirits. My friend Stewart, who used to love spinning yarns, had a theory about the origin of many of these tales. It was fascinating and I wish he'd written it down before he died because I can only remember a small part of it.

He reckoned fairies were simply people with fair-coloured hair who had originally come to Scotland from Scandinavia. For whatever reasons, they had not been welcomed and had taken to living in caves from which they would forage at night for food (watch out for fairies in the dark). He thought they might have been partial to 'magic' mushrooms (folklore tells of fairies dancing around mushrooms or toadstools) and for generations used these hallucinogens (old tales tell of travellers being given food or drink by fairies, then seeing visions, making them believe a spell had been cast on them). This, combined with inbreeding, had resulted in genetic malformations: knobbly finger joints and stunted growth. He suggested they might have developed day-blindness from living in underground caves and would have been self-sufficient, skilled in leatherwork and that sort of thing.

His old grandmother had told him that in the Highlands there was a belief that if you left out old shoes with some food, the fairies would take them away in the dead of night and repair them, returning them to your doorstep before morning. Fairies were shy people who were afraid of direct contact with others – an alternative community a bit like the travellers you see nowadays migrating to Stonehenge for the summer solstice, but without the hash, beat-up guitars or scrawny dogs they lead around on bits of old rope.

Anyway, it was a hot summer's day and as I reached Glen Shiel on the way back home there was a late-afternoon thunderstorm. It is very rare to see a really powerful thunderstorm in Scotland – it doesn't often get sufficiently hot and humid – but this one was absolutely spectacular: boiling storm clouds charged up the glen, following the road; rain battered down; forked lightning lashed out of the anguished sky and crashed on to the wet tarmac. I pulled into a lay-by to watch it and put on Jimi. Loud, very loud. *Wild thing* . . . crack!

Perfect for storms. *Voodoo child* . . . crack! And there, racing in front of the storm, desperately trying to stay ahead of its fury, was a group of motorcyclists with long, silver hair, their roaring engines screaming as they forced them into faster gears, hunched low, fleeing the tempest that was chasing them. It was as though the Devil was on their heels.

Perhaps ǝH was . . .

20

MESSING WITH THE KID

Ben Nevis

IT SHOULD REALLY BE CALLED 'CHAMPAGNE MOUNTAIN' BECAUSE THERE ARE more celebrations on it than any other hill in Scotland. It's a real *par-tay* animal; it loves company.

Ben Nevis is, of course, the best-known hill in the UK because it is the highest point between the Alps and Greenland. If you had bionic eyesight and visibility was incredibly clear, you could gaze over the whole of Ireland and the Atlantic to America, and all the way down across England and France towards Mont Blanc without the top of any other mountain troubling your view. That's a long way. If it were just a bit higher, it would break through into the permanent snowline, which would do the Scottish skiing industry a world of good.

Day-trippers have been happily hiking up and down the Ben for at least three centuries and doubtless a lot more; the notion that hundreds of years ago the locals would not walk up the hills they lived beside is baffling. Why wouldn't they want to see the view? All Hamish and his pals had to do was feed themselves and occasionally sort out invading English lager-louts who fancied their chances. They had far more leisure time than we have today; life was one long holiday, was it not? A stroll up a gently sloping mountain to a secluded summit was probably pretty common amongst horny Highland teenagers, especially if their girlfriend had a red-haired father with a sharp claymore. There are even Chinese watercolours painted in the fourth century BC that feature rock climbers, although there's no sign of pink Lycra.

In fine weather, the main path to the top of Ben Nevis is long but straightforward, in that you need no mountaineering skills. There used to be a hotel at the summit and a wee postie walked up the path to deliver mail every day – you can picture him with his sack and a Woodbine. The hotel was more or less abandoned in 1904; perhaps it was just as well – he would have been mightily pissed off if he'd had to spend his days lugging up bagfuls of advance notices of prize draws from *Reader's Digest* and blank cheques from loan companies.

Ben Nevis is typical of the largest mountain in any country, in that it attracts people with all sorts of hillwalking experience, and many with none. Sometimes, you see joggers who look like they desperately need a good feed, wearing little more than those tiny nylon shorts with the side splits, their plums swinging from side to side as they bound downhill. They pass hairy climbers, sweating underneath massive clanking rucksacks, and trade cheery banter with them. It's a very sociable place; it brings out the best in people, or most of them, at any rate.

It is not unusual to see fully geared-up mountaineers passing tourists dressed in little more than sandals and pink Pringle sweaters, doggedly plodding to the summit, a golf umbrella their only protection against sudden storms. If the sun is shining at the bottom, Bert and Mabel from Cleethorpes will pack a bottle or two of fizzy cola and a couple of Mars bars, and have a go – *come on, Mabel, we're on holiday!* – which is absolutely fine. If they want to risk hypothermia, that's up to them. Good luck to them. They usually manage to get up and back down safely, as long as they stick to the path. At weekends, there are often entire officeloads of people, from the managing director to the tea lady, all dressed in identical brightly coloured T-shirts, marching up the path to raise money for charity, many of them on a hill for the first time. When they get back down, it is heart-warming to see them, elated with their achievement, popping corks, some having just discovered a new love for the hills.

Sometimes, you see freezing, soaking, bedraggled folk shivering gratefully at the bottom after finding out the hard way how wet and miserable the weather can be up there, and that Berghaus jackets aren't just fashion accessories. There are only a few Munros where this happens – despite the impression given by the tabloids, it is very rare to see badly equipped hillwalkers, except on mountains such as Ben Nevis and Ben Lomond. In fact, it is more common to see hillwalkers carrying far too much unnecessary crap. Salesmen in outdoor shops used to be similar to some of the failed pop stars who work in guitar stores – *and what are you going to be doing with hillwalking boots?* – but no longer. They need their commission, so they're helpful; some could have even graduated from Victor Kiam sales courses.

The most famous drama of badly equipped climbers coming to grief occurred, of course, on Siula Grande, where injured Joe Simpson epically fought his way off the mountain. Joe had fallen and shattered his leg; his climbing partner had been risking his own life trying to lower him down the slope. As they got into difficulties, his partner had to the cut the rope, following which dramatic action the unlucky Joe dropped spectacularly and almost permanently down a gaping crevasse.

His pal, understandably, assumed he was dead and left him there. *Touching the Void* is the most readable climbing book ever written and none has had broader appeal. It has reached the big screen and been described by some critics as 'the best mountaineering movie ever'; it's even in video stores in Florida, a part of the world where most people have never even heard of climbing. It has made Joe a celebrity, although he told me once (at a book signing – I'm a fan too) that at times he finds it hard to deal with the fact that people get so much enjoyment out of something that caused him so much pain. He fully accepts that he and his mate, Simon Yates, were badly equipped, but they were young and short of money.

Dare I suggest that one very simple thing, something that all sensible hillwalkers carry, might have saved him a lot of agony? A whistle. Mind you, even with Simpson's considerable writing talents, the book would have lost a lot of pages and most of its appeal had it finished with, 'I dropped into the crevasse and blew my whistle to alert Simon that I was alive, but in deep shit,' or, 'As I crawled onto the glacier, I blew my whistle. Back at base camp, Simon immediately heard it and helped me stumble down to the tents.' Kind of lacks a lot of the drama.

It is easy to be smug and knowledgeable sitting drinking cappuccino in Starbucks, but there is one other wee thing that is really simple to carry into the hills that could make it easier to find you if you get stuck out overnight and your mobile phone has run out of juice. You know those flashing bicycle lights? The little red LED ones? They are tiny, but if you break an ankle, get hopelessly lost or whatever, one of them pulsing on the hill in the dark could guide mountain rescue to you better than a laser. And they take up less space than a chocolate bar. That and a whistle. Just thought I'd mention it because it is quite easy to get lost on Ben Nevis.

An article in the 1793 equivalent of *Trail* magazine notes that it should take about five hours to reach the top of the Ben and that you are likely to have stiff legs over the following couple of days. This is still true. Even back then, there was no mention of the infamous navigation risk that awaits the unwary, in much the same way that, in 2004, in one of their normally excellent route descriptions, *Trail*, rather unfortunately, mistakenly advised hillwalkers leaving the summit to follow a compass bearing that would have taken them clean over the edge of the north face.

There is a problem up there: once you get to the top, if the weather stays nice, it is easy to retrace your steps to the path back down – the 'tourist track'; if you are caught in heavy rain, a blizzard, darkness or thick mist, it is very easy to walk off the cliffs or near-vertical gullies on either side of the summit plateau. There have been many fatalities as a result of people falling down Five Finger Gully, a gaping drop below and to the left of the summit. The ground falls away towards the top of the gully and when you are tired, your brain will often subconsciously steer you downhill towards it, away from the correct direction to the path, because it feels like the easiest way. Highly experienced climbers have finished a day battling up extremely difficult climbs on the north face of the Ben only to fall to a messy end, toppling down Five Finger Gully, even though, for them, it should have been an easy stroll down the track.

There is a simple solution to this, of course, but it touches a very raw nerve with certain people. It is so easy to make this error that, over a century ago, a line of markers was built on the summit ridge to ensure that walkers found the correct way to the safe path down. In a picture taken in 1895, you can clearly see neat piles of stones with poles sticking out the top. Seems sensible. I mean, you couldn't just keep replacing postmen. The problem is that, over the years, wooden poles rot away and cairns can easily be buried by deep snow just when you need them most.

This seemed to be solved in 1995 when Fort William Mountain Rescue Team fixed posts into the plateau to clearly mark the way off. British Alcan, who owned a large part of Ben Nevis, happily contributed to the cost. The poles could have been a great help to anyone making their way down, especially if they had been unlucky enough to be caught out by the bad weather which can suddenly close in at that altitude any time of year. Lochaber Mountain Rescue, the people who get called out of their warm beds in horrendous storms to perform frequent acts of heroism on the mountain, are in favour of the poles. Professional mountain guides, such as Alan Kimber, who has 30 years' experience on the Ben, believe the poles would save lives and are a logical idea. And so you might think they would be able to breathe a sigh of relief knowing the mountain was a little safer.

Unfortunately, in Scotland there is a tiny minority of hill users who believe that they have the right to impose their views on thousands of people who enjoy the Ben. Almost immediately, a few of them, under the assertion that those who venture onto mountains should not be 'pampered' and that danger is a 'necessary' aspect of the hills, took it upon themselves to sneak up the mountain with hacksaws and cut down the poles. They have not been replaced. The John Muir Trust, which owns the summit plateau, and the Mountaineering Council of Scotland (not to be confused with the Scottish Mountaineering Club, the SMC, although some people are members of both) are well aware that someone would cut them down again and have been talking about it for years.

The MCofS is the rather grand name adopted by a group of people who call themselves the 'national governing body' of hillwalking and climbing in Scotland. Some of them are bitterly against the placing of any kind of way-marking that might help lost walkers; in their magazine, *Scottish Mountaineer*, one member has been quoted as saying that 'a few deaths are a small price to pay'. They claim markers are the 'thin end of a very big wedge' and are committed to their personal little jihad against them. Some even feel their blood pressure rise when they see thoughtfully placed little piles of stones at the side of the path, and kick them over.

During the 'big debate' at their 'Annual Gathering' of 2004, council members voted against allowing markers or cairns beside the 'tourist track'. To justify this decision, some MCofS members insist only people with mountaineering skills belong on Ben Nevis, that it is a *mountaineers'* mountain. Of course, there is no such thing; there never has been. Every year more than 100,000 people walk up the easy path to the top; the vast majority are ordinary hillwalkers, foreign tourists, people doing charity walks or families having a day out in the fresh air – only a tiny percentage are mountaineers. Considering the deaths that could result from their ruling, a reasonable person might assume that the council's decision had the backing of thousands of hill users all over the country. Now, here is the point. A total of 34 MCofS members took part in the debate and the vote to 'remove all cairns' was carried by only 20 of them.

The Ben is a very sociable mountain but there are always killjoys twitching behind net curtains desperate to spoil the fun. You might think that out of thousands of mountains in Scotland, one popular hill could have a few safety poles that might save lives, or just reduce the intense distress suffered when someone thinks they're hopelessly lost, and perhaps cut down on the number of times the mountain rescue has to be called out. Unfortunately, a determined little minority don't see it that way. If you are ever having a party and the police appear at exactly 10.01 p.m., you'll know who complained to them about the noise. But it gets even more anti-social.

There are many mountains, some just along the road from and far less dangerous than Ben Nevis, which have rusty old fence posts running all over them, which are described in the *Munro* book as being reliable navigation aids in 'thick weather'. But the fundamentalists keep quiet about that; a cynical man might say this is because only experienced Munro-baggers like themselves visit these hills.

The MCofS do a lot of very useful environmental work and will help anyone wishing to learn navigational skills, but the vast majority of people using Ben Nevis have neither the time nor the desire to become roughty-toughty mountain men.

Woolly sweaters itch too much and you'd feel such a prat wearing socks with sandals to work.

It's OK, I wrote that last bit in Jittery Joe's Coffee Shop; the double espresso has worn off, I've calmed down. The daft thing is, I don't know why they've got their woolly Y-fronts in a twist, Ben Nevis has something for everyone; there's more than one way to reach the top. Well away from the tourist path, the hidden, north-facing side has many mountaineering routes – the most famous being Tower Ridge. It's the Taj Mahal of the Highlands; if you enjoy climbing or difficult scrambling, then it will definitely be on your hit list.

The first time I climbed it was during the summer, on one of those rare perfect-weather days that you just have to grab. I had worked until mid-afternoon, then Alex and I raced to the lay-by just across from Fort Bill golf course, arriving at 5 p.m. It was a lovely sunny July night as we hiked up through scattered old Scots pine trees, ferns and flowery stuff beside a sparkling, gurgling burn – then I stopped dead when I saw the business side of Ben Nevis. Most people only ever see the huge, south-facing humpback ridge sprawling gently up from Loch Linnhe like a sleeping whale. The glowering north face is completely different – the violent relative the rest of the family try to keep quiet about.

I am willing to bet that Ben Nevis was simply the name of a local clan chief, but *The Munros* says it means 'cruel or venomous mountain' and when you see the hidden north face, you realise why. It looms over you like a huge nightclub bouncer; this side of the mountain takes no guff – from anyone. It doesn't say come on, try to climb me if you think you're hard enough. It doesn't need to. Like a street fighter, it doesn't brag. The most warning it will give you is a serious glance. If you have grown up in a city like Glasgow, you will have learned from a very young age that the guy you have to be wary of is not the shell-suited ned shouting drunken threats as he staggers along Sauchiehall Street, it's the silent guy with cold eyes and fists like 10-lb hammers. The hardman sitting alone in the corner. He ain't gonna tell you what he's gonna do to you. He'll just do it, fast as a whip. Perhaps if you are lucky, he may give you one quiet warning. If you rattle his cage, the lights will go out. No messing about, no chat. He hasn't kept his head on his shoulders by doing embroidery in his spare time. If you are smart, you will know not to screw around with him.

The north face of Ben Nevis is like Van Morrison, Jerry Lee Lewis and Noel Gallagher combined; the James Brown of the Highlands. If you're looking for trouble, you've come to the right place. It is a long row of black, vertical, sharp walls, malevolent sheer faces and plunging gullies. In summer, it is quietly hostile. In winter, you just do not screw with it. More people have been killed on Ben Nevis than the North Face of the Eiger. A friend has a picture of her husband moments before he was airlifted to hospital: it is the middle of the night, pitch-dark except for the beams of rescuers' headtorches slashing the deathly black air, but you can see he has a huge grin of relief on his face. A small but almost lethal avalanche hit him as he neared the top of the climb, but it had only broken his leg. He knew how lucky he was that his head and arse were not separated by 1,000 ft of rock.

So when I looked up and picked out the line of Tower Ridge soaring into the sky, my stomach began twitching as I walked. This is a scary place. You can feel it quite clearly. After almost two hours' plodding, we stopped at the impressive stone-built CIC hut, the only Alpine-style hut in Scotland. It is owned by the Scottish Mountaineering Club and the general public are not welcome. All over Europe, in the Alps and Dolomites, or high on most mountain ranges, you can always get a cup of good coffee and often a bed for the night in beautiful little *refugios* – in Scotland this isn't possible.

In Europe, the mountains are open to all – children and

grannies alike; people are encouraged to use them; access is made as easy as possible. Families spend pleasant weekends hiking up well-marked paths and can relax in the sun at altitudes twice the height of our dear Ben, enjoying espresso and an ice cream; it is all part of the local ethos and economy. There is none of the elitism that a few activists perpetrate on the majority of hill users in this country. Could this have something to do with the fact that mountaineering in Scotland was once a pastime of the rich?

We sat down outside the locked hut and filled up with water from a running hose that seemed to be plumbed into the side of the hill. The hut was completed in 1924, erected by Mr and Mrs Inglis Clark as a memorial to their son, Charles, who had been a member of the Scottish Mountaineering Club and was killed in the 1914–18 war. It had more locks on it than Barlinnie Prison, and an Everest base-camp pile of discarded gas bottles strewn around the back. The hut is for the use of members of the Scottish Mountaineering Club and they take ownership of it pretty seriously.

In his excellent book, *Summit Fever*, Andrew Greig tells us of the winter of 1984 when two highly experienced mountaineers were caught in one of the worst blizzards ever to hit the Highlands. The rescue services were stretched beyond their limits – five other climbers died that grim night – and conditions on the Ben were an unimaginable hell. High on the mountain, the men somehow managed to abseil off Tower Ridge where 'their lowered ropes flew up in the air like snakes charmed by the banshee howl of the wind' and, near exhaustion, crawled on hands and knees down to the door of the CIC hut. Incredibly, they were refused entry because they were not members of the SMC. *Em, not tonight, lads.* It took them another six and a half hours to stagger down in the dark through the howling wind and driving snow to safety.

To be fair to the SMC, most climbing clubs have huts somewhere, although normally down at road level, and if they didn't keep the doors bolted, they might be trashed in no time. The old Creagh Dhu club, an infamous group from Clydebank with the reputation of having the hardest climbers in the country, is an exception. They have a hut, just below the Bookle, that is left unlocked and has been there as long as anyone can remember. It is well-known; I once gave a lift to a stunned German girl who was hitching to the first available bath in the nearest hotel. She'd read about the hut in climbing books and decided that spending a night in it would be a wonderful part of the Glen Coe experience. If you take one look inside at the broken corrugated iron walls, the mouse shit, muck, rubbish, whisky bottles and beer cans, you wouldn't blame the SMC for investing in heavy padlocks.

You can't just wander into the CIC hut, although, in one of their guidebooks, the SMC let you know they have no objection to you leaning against the outside walls while you put on your climbing harness. Honest. There is no hint of irony or sarcasm. So, there you go. Members of recognised climbing clubs can book some of the beds in advance. The only people who are said to have flouted the rules were members of the Creagh Dhu. If any snobby SMC arsehole wanted to throw them out in the rain, they were perfectly welcome to try. But that may just be a romantic tale.

In summer, Tower Ridge is a long scramble, seductively beautiful but potentially dangerous; if you are at all unsure about how you feel on very exposed rock, then it is definitely advisable to have a climbing rope, and harness and belay stuff. We couldn't be bothered with the extra weight – it would just be a faff – and, as usual, I believed Alex when he told me the climb would be easy.

For once, he was right. It is about a three-hour clamber with sensational views from the not-too-daunting ridge to the point that tends to be the most intimidating. Tower Gap lurks at the end of a long bridge of dark rock linking Tower Ridge to the main Ben Nevis face. Dangerous as a cut-throat razor, it drops straight down for about 1,000 ft on either side. It would be horrible in rain. We were lucky, it was a beautiful night. Just as we reached it, we were treated to a tropical sky as the sun slid down into the sea. We sat at the gap, our feet dangling over the edge; it was warm and the world was a damn fine place to be.

Once across the gap, it is a short hoof up to the summit, and we lazed around there until after midnight watching satellites and all sorts of stuff sail around the night sky. When I am an old fart in some nursing home, hoping the nurses will be wearing low-cut tops and mulching up my food nice and soft, these are the sorts of moments I'll recall with a sigh. I'll be very glad that of the thousands of days in my life, I spent one of them doing Tower Ridge.

In winter, of course, Tower Ridge is a whole different reality show. Although it was first climbed in winter in 1894, there were not many subsequent ascents for some time, partly because of the First and Second world wars, when young men had greater demands placed on their time. When W.H. Murray, Dr J.H. Bell and colleagues finally succeeded in doing it in 1939, the gap had stopped many previous attempts.

The climbing equipment available nowadays makes it a much easier proposition than it was back then; ascents that took 14 hours by experts swinging long, wooden-handled ice axes, painstakingly hacking steps up the snow and ice, can now be done by amateurs like me using crampons and lightweight, curved, short axes. It can be very scary, especially Tower Gap, from where there have been countless rescues. After I climbed it in winter with Mr A.T. Mayes, Dr S.J. Osbourne and Nigel, we changed his name to No Longer Nervous Nigel. In every previous climb he had come on with us, he'd gulped at the bottom, told us we were insane, turned round and hurried straight back to the car; this time, he almost strolled up the ridge, calm as a dose of diazepam.

There is another possible hazard on Ben Nevis and while I unreservedly admit that my knowledge of Scottish mountains is

slight compared to professional mountain users, there is
something about which I feel sure I am the first to warn the
public. A danger that no amount of navigation poles could
prevent. A great white shark of the mountains, if you will;
extremely rare, but if heading your way, any contact will be
spectacularly fatal.

Imagine you are climbing a route on the north face. It is a
beautiful summer's day; the rock is perfect, dry and warm to
touch. You are deeply content. You have just made a satisfying
move that needed all your skill, linking your muscles and mind
in combined fluid motion. There is a sudden noise above. You
freeze: what is that horrible sound coming straight at you? Is it
a rock falling? No. Another climber hurtling through the air?
No. Possibly your very last thought as the dark object crashes
down towards you, obliterating all light, is *what the fuck is
that?*

Many years ago, a friend who owns a removal company,
helped by three of his employees, pushed a piano all the way
to the top. Not one of those modern lightweight wooden jobs
either, the ones that warp the minute they get near central
heating. No siree, this was a proper iron-framed German
overstrung; a real heavy old brute. When they got to the trig
point, they leaned back and unzipped cans of frothing lager in
celebration of the money their sponsored push had earned.
But, being removal men, they tilted back a few too many tins
and as sure as hell weren't going to carry the piano all the way
back down. They'd only been sponsored to push the thing *up*
the hill.

As we know, the summit ridge has all too easy access to
precipitous gullies and sheer drops, and so the casual observer
may have seen what was probably the only piano in history to
be heaved off the top of a mountain, and watched
dumbfounded as it sailed through the air, clattering and
clanging and bouncing and shattering to splinters 2,000 ft
below. Bits of the oak casing and metal frame are probably still
there; if any climber has reached an airy ledge and been baffled

by finding a piano string, an ivory key, part of a candle holder or a piece of wood with the word Stein on it, I am happy to have cleared up the mystery. They did raise quite a lot for charity, though.

Uh . . . maybe the MCofS have a point.

21

ROCKY MOUNTAIN WAY

Cuillin Ridge

CLIMBING AND PLAYING GIGS ARE VERY SIMILAR. YOU GET NERVOUS BEFORE both and, if it all goes well, feel a huge buzz at the end. Though, generally speaking, you don't get laid after a climb. Not to worry, you're too tired anyway.

When I joined the String Band, I had ten days to rehearse before we went on a week-long warm-up tour of France, then a forty-two-date tour of the UK, along with radio shows, TV in France, and small parts in a couple of movies that were being filmed. I was twenty-three. Ten days is not a long time to learn the chord sequences and all the twiddly bits, especially in a band that played, well, let's say a very varied set.

The first gig I did with the band was at the Paris Olympia. It was packed and Don McLean was our support act. Only two weeks earlier, I had been living in Glasgow in a riotous band flat with Mickey and Jake, and seen him do 'American Pie' on *Top of the Pops*. Next thing I knew, I was trembling at the side of the stage with my Fender Stratocaster, waiting to go on, watching him singing to the enthusiastic, although slightly

170

bewildered, audience about taking his 'Chevy to the levee', wherever that was; I am not sure even he knew.

Another time, we were just about to go onstage to a packed hall at Drury Lane in London. In those days, fire regulations were less strict and the price of a few drinks to various doormen clearly meant double the official capacity were crammed inside. The aisles were packed, sweat dripped from the walls; the old theatre had never seen anything like it; the atmosphere was fantastic.

Just as the hall lights dimmed and the stage went dark, and the roadies were shining their little torches to show us the way on, Mike told me Jimmy Page, probably the world's greatest all-round guitarist, was in the audience. I didn't stop shaking until halfway through the last song.

There were only a few gigs that I used to feel really nervous about – what you do in a pro band is learn the set so well you can play it in your sleep. You're not figuring it out as you go along; you think about nothing else all day. Even as I was nodding off at night, I'd run through the material in my mind. When bands do tours, they usually play a few gigs in some out of the way place, study the audience's reaction and quickly learn that what sounds good in rehearsal doesn't always work in front of an excited crowd. This lets the band finely tune the set, so they know exactly what to play, how to play it and in what order to get the best response. Virtually everything is rehearsed to the last note – even the bits that look totally off the cuff. Bands know that, with the exception of hardcore fans who follow them everywhere, not many people will see two gigs in a row, so you more or less do the same set every night in whatever town you happen to be in. This may sound contrived but works very well: you have to give the best product possible to the people who have paid to see you; you can't just fanny around and play a jam session. The ISB often did several shows at the same venue – in New York on our final tour we sold out six gigs in a row, and even then we played the same set every time. It works.

The way you deal with nervousness is to make damn sure you

know what you will be doing: rehearse your riffs so you can play them without thinking, have a basic routine you can rely on, then relax as much as you can and use it. If you are lucky, you might have a really good night and do something exceptional, but don't try anything fancy unless you are certain you can pull it off. The same applies to many things in life, especially climbing. And nowhere more so than on the Cuillin Ridge in Skye.

A complete hike along this ridge – what writers usually call a traverse – is *the* major mountaineering expedition in the UK and one of the most sought-after in the world. There is a great deal of climbing and clambering, often without ropes (there just isn't enough time to set them up every time you come to a steep bit), so if you suspect that you might be prone to vertigo, then you will find out for sure within seconds of stepping onto this sharp, black ridge. Even a window cleaner used to whistling a cheery tune outside the 100th floor of the Empire State Building could become a gibbering wreck. It is very high and very long, and, unless you are wearing red knickers and a blue cape with a large 'S' on it, usually involves an uncomfortable overnight stop – a doss – somewhere along its length. At various points along the ridge, there are little circles of stones that climbers have built to stop them rolling off in their sleep.

It is wise to train thoroughly for the ridge. I did. Joan stared at me as though I had finally lost my last faint grasp on reality as I set up my thin, ultra-light sleeping bag below the coldest, draughtiest spot in the bedroom, opened the window to let the freezing February air blast in, and lay down on the hard, stiff floor for the night. Hey, whatever it takes.

When I started hillwalking I never dreamed I'd be able, or even want to do the Cuillin Ridge. It's a big outing: up to 18 main summits, 14 of them over 3,000 ft, and never dropping below 2,500 ft over its 7-mile span. That's a lot, and I mean a lot, of clambering; something like a total of 13,000 ft – imagine climbing straight up 10 Empire State Buildings all piled on top of each other; it's almost half the height of Everest. Alex wouldn't let me near the Cuillin until he knew I could do it. Had me training for it for months, dragging me up to Glen Coe to climb things like Curved Ridge in raging storms, so that if the weather turned bad it wouldn't be a problem . . . actually, I got quite into wild-weather walking. If you take your time and are wearing the right stuff, it's a great experience: wind howling, rain almost horizontal; it takes a bit of getting used to, but the atmosphere can be supernatural, especially in the dark. You also learn to appreciate lying in bed on stormy nights, listening to gales bending the trees outside, knowing what it would be like high on dark mountains not so very far from your warm blankets.

If it's very windy, I wear ski goggles, even though they make me look a bit of a wassock. I am so short-sighted I can't even see my feet, so I have these big ones with thick prescription lenses in them. One day, the hill I had been on had been so windy it whipped my glasses off my face and they were gone for ever. I had to drive home using the goggles to see. Got a lot of strange looks on the Great Western Road. *Aw, piss off.*

We also climbed at every opportunity: during the week, I trained at the climbing wall where I constantly knackered my hands (the joints of my fingers were beginning to look like wee Yoda's from *Star Wars*); at weekends, we worked our way round Glen Coe, Glen Nevis and as many other climbing areas as possible, so that I could learn to use ropes and the other equipment we'd need as efficiently as possible. On the Cuillin Ridge, you definitely don't have time to rack your brains trying to figure out how to tie the specialised knots you need for abseiling – it's got to be so well rehearsed it becomes instinctive.

Many people regard the Cuillin as the finest ridge in the world and, partly because it gazes over the western sea, it is one of the most beautiful. It'll often take a few attempts, either because the exposure takes a lot of getting used to or because of rain – Skye can be a bloody dreich place. Alex has been doing it every summer for years and I'd tried it with him once before, but we'd been washed off the damn thing. When we realised we were climbing through what had more or less become a waterfall, we called it a day.

The second time I tried it, Alex and I did it from north to south, the opposite of the normal route; there is more climbing that way, and, what the hell, it would be a change from the last time. We started at the Sligachan Hotel, where they have midges that are just dying to meet you. You have to keep moving, but it is tempting to stop and watch Japanese tourists yelping as they do the dance of a thousand nips while they try to take a few quick snaps with their Nikons.

We clambered up into thick, clammy mist to the narrow ridge leading up to Sgurr nan Gillean on the other side of the mountain from the walkers' path, roped up and climbed across blocks of rock dangling above a huge dark chasm, then padded up a steep, greasy slab to the summit. The weather was piss awful: that dreary, unremitting mountain drizzle that is nature's equivalent of clinical depression. We climbed back down onto the ridge and scrambled up to the top of the next peak, Am Basteir, passing some dripping, chubby-arsed, middle-aged men and women who were being led in a very slow roped-up convoy by an irritable English guide.

There are eleven Munros on the ridge, which can be climbed separately or in groups of two or three, and anyone who is aiming to get round all the Munros is, of course, keen to do them. They are far more difficult than hillwalking on the mainland; the Cuillin mountains are composed of rough volcanic rock, mercilessly steep with precipitous ledges and hideous drops everywhere; even compasses don't work very well there, it's almost as if they've taken fright. They are really mountaineering adventures and there are guides who lead clients along the various sections, breaking the ridge down into several outings. Some of them are excellent and well worth hiring.

The guide's procession was moving so slowly it would be lucky to get down off Am Basteir by nightfall and everyone was clearly shitting themselves. They were not at all happy and I could see their point; they didn't even seem like hillwalkers – they looked as though they had been hauled straight out of warm offices and force-marched along part of the ridge on one of those stupid corporate team-building trips. We waited until they had stopped for a cigarette on a broader section, then nipped by them. The guide swore and muttered at us as though we were skipping the queue at the cinema, but we were running late enough as it was – one or two of these characters have a very proprietorial attitude about *their* Cuillin Ridge. In Europe, of course, it would be oh so different.

In Switzerland, Germany, Austria, France and Italy in particular, guides and climbers have, with the help of their town councils, developed what are known as *via ferrate*. Via ferrata means 'iron way'. Steel cable is bolted on to climbing routes and steep mountain paths, and people with no previous experience flock to the areas in summer to get a taste of what big-time mountaineering is all about. It is fantastic.

In the Dolomites in northern Italy, the cables were originally put up during the First World War so that troops could climb high, haul up serious artillery and then blow the shit out of enemy supply vehicles crossing to or from Austria. Boys will be boys. Every year, these routes are checked and maintained by the Club Alpino Italiano. You wear a special sort of lanyard with two karabiners at the ends and clip these into the cable as you scramble up the rock. If you are very unlucky and fall, you might break a bone, but you can't fall very far. You feel confident using this system and, when you feel safe, you can relax and enjoy climbing, thereby minimising the risk of falling. More to the point, you can't get lost – you just follow the cables and rocks with red and white paint helpfully daubed on them.

The via ferrate attract outdoor enthusiasts from all over the world. Nestling unobtrusively into hillsides are beautifully built hotels, chalets and mountain huts that were formerly only used during the ski season, but are now open all year, creating much-needed jobs for locals. The routes are carefully graded and people of all abilities have wonderful days out scrambling up massive rock faces in relative safety.

Some routes are difficult and you really need rock-climbing experience if you want unspoiled underwear; the steepness of some cliffs is absolutely mind-blowing: the Cesare at Passo Pordoi, the Tomaselli at Falzarego or the Punta Ana at Cortina, for example. There are hundreds of easier routes, comparable in difficulty to things like Curved Ridge or Aonach Eagach, that Mum, Dad and the kids can do quite easily – if they have any difficulty, just pull on the cables. There are even wire and plank bridges spanning awesome gorges and clefts between cliffs and massive rock faces. It all makes for a tremendous mountain experience, especially when many routes, such as the stunning Tridentina, high above the picturesque village of Corvara, have a superb little mountain hut at the top sitting snugly beside a turquoise lake, with a steaming espresso machine and smiling waitress waiting for you to stagger in, tired but with a huge grin on your face.

Unfortunately, there is only one via ferrata in Scotland – a coastal path in Fife. It is good fun, especially if you do it under a full moon, or, like Alex and I, are daft enough to try it at high tide, but it's nothing like the real thing. Although they are a tiny minority of hill users, some of the established climbing community are dead against allowing *any* of the thousands of mountains in Scotland to be made more user-friendly in this way. They would be apoplectic if the ridge was set up like a via ferrata, and insist that if you cannot climb the Cuillin using your own skills and knowledge, then you have no business being on it. Must be great fun at parties, these guys.

As we came down off Am Basteir, the weather was miserable, the slippery rock wet and greasy, and we realised this first section had taken us five hours; it was already two o'clock in the afternoon. I was all for calling it off; we were soaking wet – drookit – and, call me a wimp, but the thought of shivering all night high on the narrow ridge in the cold rain did not appeal to me. Clearly, if it had taken us this long to do two

Munros, the other nine on the ridge were going to take . . . *bloody hell.*

The weather girl on TV had promised good weather, though, and who could doubt her? We sat chewing birdseed bars or some such delicacy (I'd learned from the last attempt to carry as little as possible, so most of the food I brought for the two-day, uh, traverse, could be packed into a pocket). We stared into the clinging, damp mist, wondering if we should go back down, when, suddenly, it lifted a little and we could see that out over the sea there was an untroubled, vast blue sky. The forecast was for greatly improving weather and it looked as though it was heading our way. Twenty minutes later, our clothes were steaming in the sun and the clouds were disappearing fast. Perfect. *Right, that's decided it. Let's get going.*

If you are planning on doing the ridge without a guide, you need a few things. You need to be as hill-fit as possible, have some experience on other ridges so that you are not petrified by the exposure, know at least the basics of rock climbing, be able to set up abseils because you sure as hell will need them and, possibly most important of all, have a 'camel'.

Despite all the rain it gets, there is usually only one source of water on the ridge in summer and it is unreliable. You also have to know exactly where it is, although that is kind of stating the obvious. Unless you are prepared to lug a gallon drum with you, which is totally impractical, you have to sort out a water supply. The guides go up the day before their clients and stash plastic bottles in their little secret places. If you stole any of these you would, quite rightly, get your arse kicked all the way down to the road. We didn't have time to go up and hide water – we'd been working all week – so we arranged for a camel.

It is a bit unfair to call him that, but he didn't mind. He was a keen hillwalker who had almost completed the Munros and had asked if we would help him up and down the part of the ridge that tends to dismay and deter most non-climbers – the Inaccessible Pinnacle. It is a vertical blade of rock, like a shark's fin, jutting into the air from the top of one of the highest parts of the ridge. According to the 'rules' of Munro-bagging, you must touch the top of each mountain and the 'In Pin', as it is known, counts as one. It is not desperately high, but there is a massive drop down one side where the ridge falls away from under it. It is easy to climb – you could nip up it without a rope if you are used to rock climbing, but, if you're not, it can be terrifying.

The deal was that he would walk up to the foot of the pinnacle and meet us there with six litres of water. In return, I would climb it, tie him into a rope and help him up. He could touch the top, tick off the most elusive Munro in Scotland and then I would gently lower him off. Alex and I would have water for the next day and he would have his Munro forever. It was a great idea. Alex reckoned we could comfortably reach it by six o'clock.

We had lost a lot of time, but at last the sun had burnt off the final clinging haze of mist and the temperature was soaring; within another hour, we were beneath a cloudless, hot blue sky, more like that of southern Spain than Scotland. I had forgotten to add a few extra hours to Alex's estimate – he has never been much good at figuring out time – and I was so engrossed in the stupendous views as we strolled, clambered, abseiled and climbed along the ridge that I hadn't realised we were running three hours late. The sky was still a glorious blue, but the sun would go down very soon. By ten o'clock at night, we were still two long summits away from the camel; it would be suicide to continue along the ridge to him, even in the semi-darkness of Scottish midsummer.

I had given him a radio, so I called him. He'd been waiting at the pinnacle for us since afternoon and was determined to climb it. He said he was happy to spend the night huddled at the foot of it; we would meet him there next morning. He said he was a little thirsty and hoped we didn't mind if he drank some of our water. As the sun sizzled down into the ocean, we threw our sleeping bags on the ground and Alex fired up his little stove to cook some food; we were ravenous.

It isn't comfortable dossing on the ridge: it was bloody freezing and, of course, when you know you really need to sleep, it is impossible. The ridge is not easy: you have to concentrate every minute – one slip and you're gone – and it is difficult to be alert if you have been twitching all night with little stones that, in the darkness, suddenly feel like huge rocks pushing into your ribs. But, hey, what the hell, it's only one night; you just lie in your sleeping bag and relax as much as possible.

We met the camel next morning; he was shivering, having spent a cold night swinging his arms and jumping up and down to keep warm. He was starving, so we heated up a boil-in-a-bag curry for him – Alex enjoys spicy food and all night his sleeping bag had sounded like a motorbike. I'd decided to do without the searingly hot lamb vindaloo and the camel wolfed it down while I climbed the pinnacle; then he swallowed most of the remaining water he'd brought for us.

The guides have fixed a loop of steel cable around the top of the Pinnacle to save themselves time setting up abseils for the queues of clients they take up. After I'd lowered the camel off, he walked back down to Glen Brittle, smiling and burping, and we set off again, finally finishing the ridge at about six that evening, desperate for water, exhausted but exhilarated, partly because I didn't think I'd have had the stamina to do it. Usually, whenever I'd worked in the office after a sleepless night, I was bad-tempered and gulped Red Bull to think straight; it is interesting that even if you feel mentally shattered, your muscles keep working just fine.

Alex and I walked down off the ridge and at last reached Loch Coir a' Ghrunnda, Gaelic for 'lake of the totally knackered', where we stretched out in the warm sunshine. After a while, we noticed a girl on the mountainside smiling as she strolled, almost floated downhill towards the loch. She moved so gracefully, so effortlessly, that she seemed to be part of the land, merging with the hill, the sky and the shimmering water, the miracle of the human form combining with the perfection of the mountains, both belonging together. I thought of some words from a song Robin Williamson had written, *in time her hair grew long and swept the ground . . . it bore the holy imprint of her mind.* Without her, the mountains would have been barren; she gave life to the rock, and it basked in it, reflecting it back to her, as though she was the reason it was there.

I thought of friends with whom I'd played in bands; how I used to think exercise was carrying home a couple of six-packs from the off-licence. I looked at my aching hands; the rough Cuillin rock had worn away my fingerprints leaving painful, shiny skin. I lay back against a boulder, gazing up at the ridge. It had taken all of our energy, we felt as though our bodies were down to their last few calories, but instead of feeling drained I was glowing. The ridge is often described as one of the best mountaineering experiences in the world; I had done something that, not that long ago, would have been impossible for me.

There have been countless descriptions written about the Cuillin where the authors get so carried away they sound like Victorian dramatists on absinthe: 'antlered Cuillin, oh wond'rous serrated bridge of cliffs, beyond the sea of sorrow', all that sort of stuff . . . but it's not surprising. They are right.

22

MY GENERATION

Mid-life childhood

WHEN I WAS 20, I NEVER THOUGHT I'D SEE 30. AND I WOULD NEVER HAVE imagined that on my 50th birthday I'd be perched high on the freezing north face of Ben Nevis, on a winter route called Green Gully, climbing over yet another bulge of overhanging frozen snow and hacking up a deathly still, vertical sheet of ice to reach Alex, nestling in a slight hollow. He put his finger to his lips and whispered quietly to me.

'Shhh, don't shout or anything. Be as quiet as you can.'

Oh, fuck.

He pointed up. 'Look at that.'

About 80 ft higher and directly above us, a massive snow cornice hung far out from the top of the summit ridge. It was poised over our heads, balanced so precariously that it looked as though it might crash down on top of us at any moment; all it would take was a shout, the clang of an ice axe, perhaps someone above walking too near the cliff edge, or just bad luck. Instantly, the blood drained from my face and my guts began their all-too-familiar quivering. There must have been a hundred tons of snow and ice ready to collapse at any moment.

But it didn't, like so many things we worry about that don't happen. The following morning, I flopped exhausted into bed at 5 a.m. to grab a couple of hours' sleep before going back out to work. Joan thought I was insane, but there was no chance of her showing any mercy. I had a business to run and I had better get my stupid butt on the job by eight or there'd be trouble. No excuses. If I wanted to climb all night, that was up to me, but I shouldn't think for a minute I was going to take the morning off. Did I think I was still 20?

The summer before Green Gully, Alex and I had been climbing on Ben An in the Trossachs during a hot, mid-June night. We'd done four sections (actually, climbers call them pitches, although they are vertical and you can't play football on them) of lovely dry, warm rock and reached the top just as the sun was setting. I always feel good when I see the summer sky glowing red and orange and blue, still holding light after the sun has disappeared, and we stood there for a long time, watching the colours changing, coiling our ropes, dripping with sweat. It was well after two o'clock in the morning when I crept as quietly as possible into bed. At exactly seven, Joan woke me with her elbow, a little cruelly, I thought, and stared at me.

'Did you shower before you went to bed last night?'

'Eh . . . no . . . sorry . . . it was too late . . . '

'Jesus Christ, you're disgusting! Just disgusting. What a smell – I woke up and thought there was a dead animal in the room!'

There are people who think that when guys my age do these sort of things, it is the result of a mid-life crisis. Could be, but it's fun. There are men who appear to be going through some sort of panic-stricken list of must-dos before the lights go out, but I prefer to think that they are enjoying themselves after having devoted their lives to the business of bringing up a family and paying endless bills. You see guys hitting 40-something with a sudden look of panic in their eyes and rushing off to buy Ducatis, but why shouldn't they? What's wrong with them taking up where they left off in their 20s? *Get your motor runnin', head out on the highway.* The A82 is packed every weekend with middle-aged men getting a fresh taste of freedom, their bellies hanging over tight, black-leather trousers as they rocket through the glens. Good luck to them, they've earned it.

I suppose, as in everything, there are some who give the whole mid-life thing a bad name, who spoil it for the rest of us. I am convinced these are the people who just didn't get laid enough when they were young and suddenly realise what they've missed. It doesn't usually happen to people who played in rock bands in the '70s.

Admittedly, I was incredibly lucky. When I was 24, I was full of energy, slim, horny and touring the States with a world-famous band. I didn't realise how well known the String Band was over there until I was asked for my autograph in the street on my first day in New York City. That is a major turn-on. So, like many others in bands, I had a wonderful time. There are many things I didn't do I now regret, and I regret many things I have done, but enjoying being young isn't one of them.

I knew a few of the guys who played with David Bowie and they had a competition to see who could boff the most girls on a US tour. Yeah, it is pretty juvenile, but rock bands are young guys. That's the whole point of it. When 20-year-old Robert Plant screamed 'gonna give you every inch of my love', he wasn't singing about building you a nice Ikea table. Whitesnake didn't choose that name because they were planning on playing folk music. One afternoon when I was sitting in an Atlanta hotel, waiting for the tour bus to take us to the sound check, a very chirpy member of Bad Company grinned at me as he escorted two heartbreaks-on-legs up to his room. *I take whatever I want and baby I want you.* And, clearly, your pal too.

Frank Zappa was unstinting in his praise of groupies: *we want a guy from a group who's got a thing in the charts*; when you're playing in any well-known band, you get great letters from them. Admittedly, the letters to the ISB tended to run more along the lines of: 'If you are ever in Puddlewick, do drop by our little cottage and share our herbal tea and home-baked bread', but the more rock music we played, the raunchier the audiences and the better the mail. 'Hi Graham, I'm writing this as I lie in bed naked . . .' I've still got that one and it served me well on many a long winter's night.

Sometimes you even get wedding proposals. Perhaps the girls that send you them do it purely for fun because there really isn't much possibility that you will ever take your blushing new fiancée home to your parents. *Hi Mum, this is Roxy, we met when she wrote to me saying that she'd love to smear whipped cream all over my body then slowly lick it off.* Playing in a top band is everything you'd imagine it to be, and more.

You can't finish a gig in front of thousands of screaming, cheering, shouting, excited people then go off quietly to have a nice cup of Ovaltine and read *The People's Friend* before clicking off the bedside light. There are guys, though, who weren't so fortunate and really should have got out a lot more when they were young.

Like . . . we'll call him 'Mad' Mick McLutcheon, a 45-year-old traffic-planner from Whitburn or Bathgate or one of those old mining towns. Mad Mick had been wiry at one time, but loved his real ale too much and his gut was like a postman's sack. He thought every girl was panting for him and that every man wanted to fight, especially when he'd had a few drinks. He still went clubbing, would hang out with what he fondly imagined to be an enticing half-smile on his face one moment and a menacing sneer the next. Unfortunately, a few of us met him in a hotel in Fort William – he was there with one of those hillwalking clubs and he made the bar seem crowded. The expression mid-life crisis was invented just for him.

He was, of course, an Atkins-diet casualty, desperately trying to lose those extra kilos. All that protein . . . he was delusional; spent his nights in the bar harassing the waitresses, boasting about how fit he was, and his days recovering from fearsome hangovers, sweating like a malaria victim as he hauled his arse up Ben Nevis like a rhino with piles to make sure no one had put up navigation poles when he wasn't looking.

There are even self-worshipping prats that want to ban people from using bikes in the Highlands and harass Munroists by posting pompous notices in car parks, warbling on about preserving the tradition of the 'long walk-in'. Listen, Porky, most of us have to work to earn a living; we don't all have time for 'long walk-ins' and, apart from that, there are Land-Rover tracks all over the place; God forbid grouse-shooters might have to walk a little. It's only a 'tradition' because no one had invented the mountain bike. It is wonderful to cycle to the foot of a Munro, especially in the Cairngorms. No doubt about it, some guys really should have got out a lot more before they became bitter old farts.

Scotland could be the healthiest nation in the world; we live in a huge playground. Somebody told me recently that there is a higher incidence of obesity among Scottish teenagers than American kids, and that guys in many Glasgow council estates reckon they've had a good innings if they reach their 60th birthday. It is because of these kind of statistics that I get angry at those who want to keep the hills for themselves. One doesn't want to be critical of our leaders in the £400-million Scottish Parliament building, but I would love to see some of our taxes spent building all-weather paths up hills and Munros near cities – let's find ways of gradually introducing kids to mountains even if a few furious bearded-wierdies choke on their porridge.

When I visited New Zealand, I read an article in a hillwalking magazine that really made me think. I'd picked it up in Auckland airport – something to read on the short flight down to Wellington. Half the mag was filled with the usual stuff – reviews of rucksacks and boots – but there was an interview with a nurse who worked in a hospice in the any-minute-now wards looking after those about to depart. She wasn't a famous Alpinist or one of those so-called mountain sportswomen, but she made more sense than any motivational guru. She just pointed out that she would get out on the hills – in NZ, they call it tramping – as often as possible. She said that when you see patients who would give anything if they could only walk to the door to get a breath of fresh air, it seemed criminal to have a healthy body and not use it. On the way back home, I saw obese people in LA who had eaten themselves into wheelchairs, who were now physically disabled as a result of shovelling down endless junk food. Then, when visiting a friend at Gartnavel Hospital in Glasgow, I watched post-operative amputees rubbing their bandaged stumps as they lit cigarettes in the cold wind, sucking down the smoke as if their lives depended on it.

You don't know what you've got till it's gone.

23

FREEBIRD

Champoluc, Italy

AT LONG LAST, MORE THAN 20 YEARS AFTER STARTING OUT WITH MICKEY, humping crappy old oak sideboards for beer money, the business had cracked it. It was doing really well: we had survived countless hassles and setbacks, getting a little stronger every time, and had grown a little more every year. I had been able to claw the money together to buy a huge modern storage facility that was recognised as one of the best in Britain – inside, we even built a replica of a house, in which we set up the only training school of its kind in Scotland. Through the British Association of Removers, we could issue government-approved formal qualifications. Some of the biggest names in the business were sending staff to us for courses; companies that, at one time, wouldn't have given me a job sweeping their yards.

I was invited to join the refined gentlemen who were the board of directors of Britannia Movers International, now a major company and probably the largest moving group of its kind in Europe. The board held regular meetings near Stansted Airport from where low-cost airlines do daily flights to Turin.

Elbow your way on to the plane, fight your way to a non-pre-assigned seat, be grateful that they don't use benches with ropes for seat belts, whatever you do, don't drink the coffee, and you are on your way. Within an hour's drive of the airport, you are in some of the finest ski country in the world. It was wet and windy in Scotland, so I didn't have to think about it. I could cruise through the board meeting then nip over to Italy for four days on the slopes. A quick call to Alex – he'd meet me at Stansted in time for the 5.30 flight. I got a few strange looks when I wandered into the boardroom wearing my ski clothes, but what the hell, I could only carry so much and the airline would show no mercy if my bag was overweight.

As it happened, Alex missed his flight from Prestwick despite a heroic struggle. He really has to get that time shit together. He should have been a drummer; they live in a different continuum. John Gilston's playing was faultless, but in real life his notion of time was, like Alex's, completely different to the rest of the worlds. I don't care as long as Alex buys the coffees.

He called me on his mobile, out of breath and out of luck. The flight from Glasgow had left. He would try again next day. I went on ahead, took a cab from Turin airport and skied all next day at Pila, then met up with him in Aosta. Next morning we headed off to Champoluc, a huge tri-valley ski area that, so far, the package companies don't use because there are only a few smallish hotels nearby. The infrastructure is not developed enough for that all-important critical mass footfall, or whatever bullshit they call it, but excellent for people who want to ski without having to spend half their time queuing for the lifts.

We'd had a fabulous day and were standing high up the mountain, big cheesy grins on our faces, leaning on our poles at the top of the long easy runs that sail down perfect snow to a cappuccino at the Hotel California, a hand-built labour of love in oak and pine just a little up the hill from Champoluc village. Above us, the sky was a deep blue, snow crystals sparkled like diamonds at our feet and we gazed across black jagged summits to Mont Blanc, behind which the sun was setting like a welcoming winter fire, throwing a warm amber glow onto the towering white pinnacle of the Matterhorn. The pistes were deserted; we had the whole mountain to ourselves. It was so good to enjoy views like this without having to stagger uphill laden with ropes and crampons and ice axes and rucksacks that felt like sacks of potatoes, dragging you down, sending torrents of hot sweat coursing down butt-cheek gully, where it froze and chilled you to the bone as soon as you stopped to catch a deep breath of cold air. Or quivering as you climbed, ducking falling lumps of ice while you tried, for some dumb reason, to hack and kick up yet another dodgy, desperate you-swore-you'd-never-do-this-again near-vertical horror story of a Scottish winter ice gully.

This was so much easier. We could enjoy the sunset, then, with the sound of the Stones blasting in our headphones – *ah know it's only rock and roll but ah like it* – cruise back down at dusk, below the now-silent ski lifts to the twinkling lights of the village way down in the valley, to leisurely deep steaming baths in our rooms. Sometimes, life can be damn good.

The following year I was asked to be chairman at a national conference in Edinburgh – a little different from my rock and roll days. As I stood in my immaculate suit in front of the huge gathering, welcoming delegates from all over Europe and introducing keynote speakers, I couldn't help but grin when I recalled that 20 years earlier, in a hotel just around the corner, I had launched a television set into orbit . . .

24

DRIFT AWAY

Torridon dreams

IT IS FANTASTIC TO SNAP ON A GOOD PAIR OF HEADPHONES AND TAKE ALL THE music you want into the hills. We are so lucky to be living at a time when this is possible. We are also incredibly lucky that in Scotland we have a place called Torridon.

There is a TV programme on the go called *CSI: Miami*. At the time of writing, it is, we are told, the most-watched show on earth. It uses as its signature tune part of Pete Townshend's 'Won't Get Fooled Again'. The only problem is that Pete's music is so powerful that, after hearing it, I need about ten minutes to settle back down enough to follow the story, by which time it's too late; I have no idea what is happening.

Future historians will look on the '60s and '70s as a renaissance, a golden age when more people became musicians than at any other time in history. Everyone wanted to learn; for a while before I joined the ISB, I used to teach guitar and one small advertisement would bring queues to my door. Mind you, when some parents stepped inside the band flat – amps, beer bottles and uninhibited girls strewn everywhere – they often took little Tarquin elsewhere to continue his musical education. The kids loved it, though. I had them playing with their teeth in no time.

For ten years after The Beatles released 'Love Me Do', music shops couldn't get enough instruments; it was a hugely creative time. OK, a great deal of it was driven by testosterone and the fact that a guitar was a passport to getting laid – this we know – but a lot of music was written that is as good as anything by the classical composers. 'Won't Get Fooled Again', for example. Listen closely to Pete's rhythmic use of guitar chords; they are so bloody powerful. He sounds like a modern-day Mozart, driving the whole thing along, building one hell of an atmosphere.

I don't know if it is any different now, but when I was at school music lessons were torture. I remember being belted by a music teacher because I was gazing out of the classroom window at winter storm clouds looming over a tree as we were listening to Beethoven or Vivaldi or someone. I felt the music perfectly reflected what was going on outside; it was part of it. He just thought I wasn't paying attention. Whack! If he wasn't swiping the kids with his heavy wooden ruler, he'd be pushing his face up close – his breath smelled like a hot compost heap – rapping our desks with his fingers, rattling out rhythms that he expected us to identify. Wrong! Whack! Even worse, he dragged each shaking pupil out in front of the class, hit a note on the piano and told the kid to sing it. So embarrassing – wasn't puberty enough? My throat closed completely and I was labelled tone deaf. Whack! Actually . . . he was probably right.

The thing is, we loved music, even though he almost knocked it out of us. All kids love music, they breathe it. They love the rhythms, the rise and fall, the flow, the poetic language, the whole *feel* of music. You see them walking to school listening to CD players, iPods, whatever; everywhere they go, they are attached to earphones, their mobile phones ring out little tunes; they can't function without it. At home, they turn it up so loud that cracks appear in the plaster; I think it's wonderful they enjoy it so much. I loved to hear the floorboards shaking loose in my sons' bedrooms as heavy bass notes pounded through the house.

Ancient philosophers revered music, believing it to be a gift from the gods, coming from some great cosmic source. Pythagoras was a very good lyre player and reckoned music could be used to heal the sick, although this was a long time before ear-bleeding Motorhead gigs. He discovered that music followed mathematical progressions that seemed the same as those that govern the movement of stars and planets.

If you have ever played with a good jazz musician, you might notice that they seem to hear music differently. It's actually very interesting. In jazz, there is no such thing as a bum note, it is the next note you play that determines whether the first 'works' or not. Good jazz players seem to hear in a way that allows them to play bizarre progressions that are in key; they seem to hear the intervals between notes differently from the rest of us. When they play a note, they instantly 'hear' other notes that will 'resolve' the first one, that will make it sound 'right', in other words, in tune. They seem to 'see' the notes as well as hearing them, a bit like balancing both sides of a mathematical equation.

When you listen to moments of genius in music, you get the feeling it is part of something else, the tip of some celestial iceberg. Every so often, as in the '60s and '70s, something happens and things are never the same again. 'Won't Get Fooled Again' sounds very simple, but listen more closely; even Hendrix didn't use chords and rhythms like Townshend. It is amazing that so many different styles of sound can be pulled out of a piece of wood with six strings stretched across it.

Hendrix was the master of psychedelic rock guitar; no one had ever played what he could wring out of a Strat. People thought his solos came straight out of the cosmos, although LSD might have had something to do with that. He was intuitive. 'Purple Haze', for example – the song is in the key of

E, yet he starts it in B flat. Fortunately, he didn't go to Hyndland School. Whack!

What about Eric Clapton? In the '60s, he recorded 'Stepping Out' with John Mayall. Shortly after the intro, he slams his finger onto the G at the 12th fret of his Les Paul, pouncing on it like a cat onto a ball, squeezing out a single soaring sound, using his amp to make it sing above the band in one beautifully timed, sustained note. No one has ever used feedback so perfectly: a combination of the guitarist vibrating the note and the guitar pick-up 'hearing' it coming from the amplifier and sending it back to it, causing a sound loop; something not taught in any school music class. But this is what is amazing. He had only been playing for about five years, about the same length of time it takes most people to learn how to tune a bloody guitar; he was barely out of his teens. Even before he formed Cream, you could see 'Clapton is God' painted on the walls in London Tube stations.

There was so much happening in music in the '60s and early '70s. Young Keith Richards, once described as the 'world's most elegantly wasted human being', took the old blues tunings from the Mississippi and put together the guitar part for 'Honky Tonk Woman'. It's full of subtle little runs and riffs; no one had ever played electric guitar like it and countless rock-guitar classics have come from that one song.

And tell me you don't feel a rush of energy whenever you hear Paul Kossoff's power-chords, most of them only three bloody notes, for God's sake. If they don't make you move every time you hear 'All Right Now', then you are ready for the dominoes-and-Scrabble lounge. Doctors should use that song instead of reflex hammers. You twitch to it, *great, you're still alive, pal. Next!*

All that music had to have a source. Did these guys come up with those chord changes and riffs by accident? What was the driving force behind it, behind all music? Was it inside or outside them? Jimmy Page, probably the most creative guitarist of them all, was deeply involved in the black arts, although he

193

said it might have been the other way round. He wasn't using them; they were using him. Where did 'Dazed and Confused' come from? Listen to 'Kashmir'. Bloody hell, how does that make you *feel* – where does it take you?

It is fantastic to listen to Mozart, The Who, Zep, the Stones or whoever when you are out in the mountains. We live in privileged times – we can slip on a good pair of headphones and take all the music we want into the hills. Or perhaps it's there already . . . especially in a place called Torridon.

Rain should never be a deterrent to hillwalking, but there is one place in north-west Scotland that, above all, you have to see in perfect weather: Torridon. When you go there, you feel a unique atmosphere, something very difficult to explain. It is as though momentous events happened long ago here among the oldest mountains on earth. Even those dreary authors who write about hillwalking with as much romanticism as a car-repair manual have commented on this strange aura. It is haunting.

To climb Beinn Alligin in the heart of Torridon in perfect weather is to be one of the most fortunate people on the planet – there are so many countries where it isn't possible to wander freely. It is a beautiful mountain with several summits linked by a high, long dragon-like narrow ridge. When you look at the ancient peaks around you, erupting straight up from the flat ground below, it is almost like being on an alien planet . . . you have to experience it yourself. The area is mesmerising in any weather, but if you are lucky enough to be bathed in warm sunshine beneath a crystal-clear sky, it is simply magical.

Sometimes a bit of dreaming is good – too many people are too damn serious about life. If you spend every day dealing with the harsh reality of earning a living, perhaps it is a good idea to think about the stuff that lawyers don't know about, that accountants can't count. It can't hurt. It's good to believe in the Loch Ness monster, it's good for the soul. Sometimes it makes a lot more sense than being crammed on the Tube, deep below the ground, hurtling along the Central Line, everyone trying to avoid eye contact, as if by being there, they are all guilty of something. And nowhere do dreams come more easily than Torridon.

There is a mountain you can gaze at from Beinn Alligin that looks as though it's had the top sliced off, almost as if ancient engineers cut through it, creating a perfectly flat summit. Yeah, yeah, I know there is a sensible geological explanation, but so what? Part of the joy of sitting at the top of a mountain is being able to forget the sensible things in life, at least for a while.

Or is the atmosphere more ominous? There are places in the world, the Colosseum for example, where, if you close your eyes and breathe gently, you feel certain you can imagine the pain, hear the screams and smell the blood of the sacrificed. If you are open to these notions, you might sense that something happened in Torridon . . . it may have been a place of evil, of human struggle, of forces of dark magick long, long before the Vikings or Picts came to Scotland.

Or it may have been a place of supreme wisdom, where a race of beings had learned to live in peace, to simply *be* with one another. It is impossible to know what, but something happened in Torridon. You can feel it, especially when you are at the top of Alligin.

When Alex and I climbed it, the weather was perfect. It was October, but as warm as August. You can walk up a path or scramble up rocky outcrops called the Horns. The view from the top is hypnotic; you look far out to the mystical islands and up the coastline, which seems devoid of any sign of habitation. For some reason, you don't feel as though you are in Scotland, there is something so strange about it; there is something very unusual about this place.

In Torridon, perhaps there is lost music. If you are in almost any city, you will hear the hum of a nearby motorway. At some point in the future, when the traffic has gone, that hum will become inaudible to human ears, but does that mean it has gone? Sound is transmitted by molecules vibrating – perhaps they are still vibrating long after we cease to hear them. It is easy to sense that in the prehistoric land of Torridon, there is music that sounded long ago, before any of our ancestors lived there. Could this be what we feel in that landscape, as it lingers still? Is it the last sound of a long-vanished time?

Perhaps the first sound in the universe was not a big bang but a perfect chord. Is all music today a part of it, a fragment, a reminder of that first moment? Perhaps one sublime sound gave birth to all others when it shattered and created time. If that music exists as a trace, if there is still a faint echo of what it was, somehow shimmering as a memory among the oldest mountains of ancient earth, if you can hear or simply sense it anywhere, it will be in Torridon. Or perhaps Torridon is simply awakening long-forgotten dreams and lost chords you have within you.

Go and listen. Before the music fades for ever.

25

MEET ON THE LEDGE
Why climbers climb

CLIMBERS LOVE TO CLIMB.

When they decide to get married, semi-pro musicians are often asked to give up playing, forget that lifestyle, *it's time to grow up*. Every famous band has at least one member who left his childhood sweetheart when she wouldn't move to London or LA; within weeks, she married the sensible architect from round the corner, while he went on to write angst-ridden, gold-selling records about it.

The same thing happens to many climbers, but fortunately they don't get to bore the crap out of the rest of us by churning out mournful hit singles. I have a pal, a gentle, quiet guy who hates any kind of confrontation. His wife is less than accommodating about his love of rock climbing, but only because she worries about him. Every weekend, no matter how perfect the weather, she would find some vital trip he had to make, some expedition to Sainsbury's or Ikea, or a visit to a long-forgotten aunt – anything that would keep him out of his climbing harness. One day, she told him she would be popping over to Paris with a few friends for a weekend shopping trip and he could hardly keep still. He called me every night, bubbling with enthusiasm over the routes we would be free to do that weekend. Just as he was dropping his wife off at the airport, she handed him a long and detailed checklist of home improvements that she demanded he complete by her return.

That night, as soon as he had finished work, he raced to B&Q, then immediately came to collect me, his eyes sparkling, leaping from foot to foot as he rang my doorbell. I had my usual freshly delivered pizzas in my hands – I loved to scoff one with my sons on Friday nights while we watched a DVD – but he didn't want to waste time. He hauled me into his car, shoving aside tins of paint and lumps of wood – we could eat as he drove.

Within half an hour, we reached a cliff not far outside Glasgow, feeling like school kids on the first day of summer break as we swarmed all over it until almost eleven o'clock, when the last hint of June light finally disappeared. Early next morning, he was back at my door and I noticed he had paint on his hands and the smell of turps on his clothes. He'd been up all night, would I mind driving? He snored contentedly for the hour and a half it took to reach a great climbing spot just outside Dunkeld, where we scampered up and down the rock until dusk, then guzzled fish suppers. He slept all the way back to Glasgow.

I was wakened by his car horn outside my bedroom window at 7 a.m. the next morning. If we left *right now*, we could make the ferry to Arran. *Hurry.* Great climbing on Arran; there was a route he'd been wanting to do for years. *The weather's brilliant, let's go.* I noticed his eyes seemed to have trouble focusing and there was the pungent smell of paint-stripper on his clothes, the same ones he'd been wearing since Friday. His hands had three different colours of paint smeared on them: he'd been working straight through the night stripping the hall banister. Joan gave me one of her pitying looks as I pulled on some clothes, and grabbed the ropes and clanky climbing gear I'd left the night before in its usual place – all over the hall floor. Outside, my pal was warming up by climbing a lamp-post. We made the ferry with two minutes to spare.

Climbers love to climb. It is a very physical thing.

Probably no other sport has such variety. There are so many different styles of climbing, from short routes on local outcrops to long expeditions battling up vast north faces on remote mountain ranges in parts of the world that are difficult to even pronounce. Regardless of what you are doing, the basic idea is the same: start at the bottom and climb to the top. Oh, and try not to fall while you're at it.

There are climbers who enjoy being in a life-and-death situation and managing, by skill and strength, to climb out of it. It has to be said, though, that many of them are fucking crazy. Some climbers are weird people, withdrawn and intense, only at home when they are waking up on their little porta-ledges, which they sleep on as they dangle 2,000 ft up a cliff. If the danger of extreme climbing is not enough to get their juices going, they even travel to places rife with terrorists, where they have the additional threat of being kidnapped just to spice things up.

Many climbers are very relaxed people: they are fit and healthy through a sport they love, and have faced scary situations which have taught them not to let the normal upsets of life annoy them too much. You can't worry about anything else when you are balancing on a little piece of rock over a plunging abyss, and the relief you feel after an epic struggle is more intense than anything you might experience in other sports – a badminton game, for example.

But not all climbing involves danger. Some of the hardest climbing in the world, called bouldering, is less risky than playing football in the local park. Bouldering is hugely popular and similar to traditional climbing in the same way snowboarding is to skiing. Mountains often have huge boulders lying below them and because they are usually not very high, no ropes or other equipment are needed to climb them. Many people regard this as the purest form of climbing: only the climber and the rock. You don't even need to hike into the countryside; there are many urban bouldering areas, such as Dumbarton, or the most famous, Fontainebleau, which is not far from Paris. Bouldering usually requires exceptional skill. Many of these huge stones have been worn almost smooth over thousands of years and are intensely difficult to climb, but if you fall you will land on nice soft grass or on the padded crash mats that you can buy in climbing shops; some guys throw an old mattress on the ground.

Apart from being physically demanding, there is also a great deal of thought and strategy involved in climbing: some fanatics doggedly 'work' a climb (what they call a 'project') for months until they can do it. One of the UK's top climbers, Paul Savage, spent a year on a boulder 'problem' rated as the most difficult in Scotland. Not long ago, if you were seen in a field trying to climb the same boulder day after day, the farmer would have called in the guys with the knowing smiles and long syringes.

Over the years, climbers have developed extremely clever, and helpful, ways of grading routes, from boulders to mountains, so that you know what to expect before you launch yourself at a climb. It is very simple; you either manage to climb something or you don't, but if you practise really hard, sometimes you can learn the intricate little moves you need to succeed on a particular route, perhaps move up a grade or two.

The great thing is that everyone climbs to their own degree of difficulty; the sense of achievement is the same. Average climbers, like myself, get as big a kick out of climbing something, well, averagely difficult, as a young rock-god gets on some desperate overhanging cliff, or a boulder that is as smooth as marble. You feel good when you manage a climb that you've stood staring at with your legs trembling, you have achieved something. Climbers love to climb because of the unique physical demands of the sport combined with the intense concentration required; it uses everything you've got.

But there is another reason.

26

STAIRWAY TO HEAVEN

Olta, Spain

I ALWAYS HAVE TO LEARN THINGS THE HARD WAY.

The wiring at gigs is much safer nowadays, but many venues used to be death traps. When I was 19, I was so badly electrocuted I escaped death by a few seconds. I had a guitar in one hand and a microphone in the other, and caused a short circuit – a big one. All my muscles contracted and I couldn't let go. The pain was horrendous; someone later measured the jolt at 1,000 volts – every molecule in my body felt as if it was exploding and I toppled face-first onto the stage. I can recall exactly how it felt and what happened.

I looked down, terrified, helpless as the excruciating, unbearable pain ripped through my flesh, killing it. I realised that I was about to die; there was nothing I could do. I could hear my voice screaming, then gradually trailing off, falling silent. Suddenly, I was annoyed at my stupidity for letting this happen, for causing this harm to myself. I was watching my body die, a body that had been *me*, but soon would be dead and useless. But there was something else, something strangely familiar about all this; I *knew* this feeling.

I realised I was somewhere above my body, watching it die. It was almost over now. The pain was changing; I could feel my body surrendering, slowly closing down as if drifting to sleep. That body had been me . . . or so I'd always thought. But I was here, watching it give up its final breaths of life. I felt sad, so terribly sorry for the people I would leave behind.

Somehow, I had a distant memory, a feeling that this had happened to me many times before. In another few seconds, I would be dead. I was dying and yet . . . I *knew* this feeling.

At the last instant, a friend managed to cut the power. The pain drained from my body and suddenly I was back inside it. I leapt up, throwing the microphone as far away as possible. There was a smell of burning . . . I looked at my hand and was rushed to hospital. That night, I walked down Sauchiehall Street grinning, just grinning. I had never seen lights so bright, never felt so alive or sensed vibrant energy from so many people as I walked among them. But, most of all, I remembered *knowing* that feeling.

Sometimes, when I've been climbing, I get that feeling once more.

W.H. Murray, the pioneering Scottish climber of the 1930s, did a great deal to revive the sport after the First and Second world wars. He was captured in the desert during the Second World War after an encounter with an SS officer which turned out to be fortunate under the circumstances. Murray had remarked that the desert at night was 'as cold as a mountain-top' and the German, realising he was a fellow Alpinist, treated him as a long-lost friend and shared a beer with him, which was a lot better than having his brains shot out.

Murray wrote his bestselling book *Mountaineering in Scotland* while in a prisoner-of-war camp. Not to be critical, but reading Murray's accounts of climbs is a bit like running your finger down the minutes of Law Society meetings: they tend to be dreadfully formal. Of course, he writes very well, but he grew up when Latin was compulsory in school, and Biggles and

Robert Louis Stevenson provided schoolboys with nightly drama as they read in bed under a dim yellow torchlight. Not much wanking material there, but they liked these books as much as teenagers nowadays enjoy steamy magazines like *FHM* or *GQ*.

Even comics in those days were better written than most of today's newspapers. Nobody was described as being 'gobsmacked' or 'gutted' and the editor of the *Glasgow Herald* paid ten shillings to any reader who spotted a spelling error. Something awful must have happened in schools around 1980. Whenever we received job applications, it was possible to guess the guy's age by whether he could fill out the form or not.

When I read Murray's books, I find my lips moving like a two-toothed Arkansas dirt farmer. His fellow climbers are referred to by their formal appellations: Dr J.H.B. Bell, T.D. McKinnon or, more briefly, simply Scott and Laidlaw. There's no 'Crazy Mayzie', 'Mental Dental Dave', 'Nanuck of the North', 'Dangling Derek', 'Lyn the Grin', 'Himal Al', 'Manky Malc and his Pervmobile', 'Fearless Frances', 'Bonehead' or 'Shagger Richards' in Murray's literature. You can picture his climbing colleagues straightening their ties and pulling up the collars on their tweed jackets before pressing onwards into the blizzard. *What-ho, old chap.*

But he did write beautifully. There is an interesting theory that parallels the decline of education (one in three prisoners in England can't read) with the rather more relaxed attitude in today's pop songs. Pre-Beatles, almost all pop music was composed by professional songwriters who worked 9 to 5 at their pianos in little smoky studios, tenderly crafting lyrics for the stars. Idols assured you in those days that when they 'gave their heart it would be completely'. Frank Sinatra admitted that he 'may not be the man some girls think of as handsome' and, despite hanging out with many heavy-set Italian friends, sang that he was, in fact, just 'a little lamb, lost in the wood', crooning that he was searching for someone to watch over him.

Compare these to Trent Reznor with his disarmingly honest

line, 'I wanna fuck you like an animal', or the Notorious BIG with his frank monologues about 'finger fucking' his dream date. Or the modern-day crooner Tenacious D, who sings, some might say unromantically, that he will happily 'shoot his juice into your caboose'.

By comparison, even the Stones were fairly restrained. On their first album, they captivated an unsuspecting world by covering an innocent Nat King Cole number, encouraging us to get our kicks on Route 66, but quickly set out their stall with 'I Just Wanna Make Love To You'. Then Brian Jones's bottleneck guitar slid seductively into Slim Harpo's 'King Bee' with the unambiguous request to 'let me come inside'; from then on, things would never be the same again.

Nowadays, even mainstream pop has no inhibitions; there was some half-naked female vocalist on TV the other night inciting the audience to 'suck my fucking titties'. Judy Garland wouldn't have put it quite like that, but who could refuse? Even The Beautiful South had their disarmingly wholesome female vocalist warning her fortunate friend: 'She'll grab your sweaty bollocks . . . don't marry her, fuck me'. Maybe she's angling for a part in the rap version of *Mary Poppins*.

Murray is therefore a gentle reminder of less direct times. He gives us, unfortunately sparingly, a hint of spiritual release that might be reached through climbing. While most books on the sport are almost interchangeable, trotting out the usual endless clichés, Murray brings some beautiful language to the mountains.

From its earliest publications, mountaineering literature has been written about boys going off on expeditions like armies marching to war; as author David Roberts neatly points out, climbers 'laid siege to a mountain', they 'attacked' it by way of 'weaknesses in its defences'; reaching the summit was seen as a 'victory' or a 'conquest'. Britain's best-known climber, Chris Bonington – Sir Chris, to you and me – was a commissioned officer in the army, a tank commander, no less. When he climbed Everest, he planned it with military precision, which contrasted nicely with a couple of Scots guys years earlier who'd attempted it while lugging a dead sheep on their shoulders for food.

In contrast, Murray recognised that sometimes it is possible to achieve enlightenment through climbing. After his famous winter ascent of Tower Ridge, he wrote:

> While we walked slowly across the plateau, it became very clear to me that only the true self, which transcends the personal, lays claim to immortality. On mountains it is that spiritual part that we unconsciously develop. When we fail in that all other success is empty; for we take our pleasure without joy . . . At last we turned and went down like fallen angels, with an ever-mounting reluctance, from a spiritual paradise to the black pit of Glen Nevis.

In his last published work, Murray talks of how, in the PoW camp, he was selected by another soldier who invited him to embark on a spiritual path. Unfortunately, Murray does not give us more than a few clues about the road he travelled, other than stating that the ideal consciousness is mindfulness of only the present moment, which, I suggest, is a pretty difficult concept to communicate to most of us with 35-year mortgages and the rest of the impositions of modern living.

This is not intended in any way as criticism of the great man, but it is a shame that he devoted so much space – especially in his final book – to descriptive prose about the Himalayan landscape and rhododendrons, and not more to his spiritual journey. Perhaps he believed the pursuit of enlightenment was really only of interest to a small minority of climbers; possibly he felt that those people seeking the path would find their way to it.

People like Alex climb, walk, whatever, for spiritual reasons. On every hill he climbs, he pauses just before sunset amid what he calls 'the settling', when the weather of the day calms as if it is resting for the night, and he gazes to the west, to Westernesse, and smiles quietly, happy just to be there. He loves to snowboard and goes off alone into the back country – he'll tell you what he is seeking: to 'surf the mystical wave'.

Neil McGeachy is a young hardbody who can spend the entire night 'trolleyed' and on the pull in Glasgow clubs, grab a short nap in his beat-up car, then dance up vertical, almost blank rock. He was invited to join the Creagh Dhu and went off to do a winter-climb with them, then realised that his borrowed crampons were not designed for the soft 'bendy' boots he'd got from a friend. *Fuck it*. He stuck them to the boots with plumber's tape and climbed a desperate ice route on Ben Nevis.

Neil can climb routes that would be impossible for most climbers, but difficulty is not what motivates him – he loves easy routes as much as the technically fearsome. He isn't competing with anyone. It is the act of climbing itself that is important; the feeling of balance of mind and body working perfectly together. Like Alex, Neil climbs for spiritual reasons. These guys are not West End dilettantes surrounded by organic muesli and free-trade decaffeinated coffee. They are hard climbers.

For eight months, I had been deep in negotiations with three different companies who wanted to buy the removal business. I was very keen to sell, but I had to make sure that the deal was absolutely right or I'd spend the rest of my life regretting it. I am very bad for looking back and trying to rewrite history when I feel I have made a mistake, but I felt very close to the ideal sale. It was too important to take chances; I had to make sure there was nothing that I'd overlooked. If I got this right, I'd never have to look at another removal van; if I didn't, I'd be spending the rest of my working life listening to the clatter of oily engines. At stake: everything.

I was now in the final stages with the potential buyer's big-time London lawyers and I'd been reading, amending and rereading fresh drafts of the complicated, 128-page contract every day for weeks. Suddenly, I noticed I had lost at least 12 lbs after pacing the streets every night, turning over clause after clause in my mind. This was crazy. I needed to get away somewhere to try to get a little perspective.

Neil is a funny guy, really funny; the ideal person to take my mind off the endless meetings with solicitors and accountants, so we nipped out to Alicante on a last-minute flight for a few days' climbing in the sun. I first met him at a climbing-wall staff party when he got up to sing a spot of karaoke. He sang 'My Way', but kept shouting and swearing between the lines, pretending he had Tourette's syndrome. It was hilarious; sick, but hilarious. Clearly, this was not a boring person. Actually, we nearly missed the flight. Neil hadn't grasped that you have to get to the gate *before* the departure time and it was only because I assured the check-in girls he would appear at any moment that they didn't heave our rucksacks onto the tarmac. Well, that and the fact I told them I was his social worker and I shouldn't have let him wander off. Could you think of a better lie on the spot? They were very understanding.

We had just finished climbing at Olta on the Costa Blanca, a lovely tree-lined mountain that overlooks the Mediterranean. We had done a dozen or more routes that day and had been the only climbers on the white limestone rock. Sometimes you find yourself in a rhythm; your body becomes a living metronome, your breath a gentle pulse, quietly ticking off the beats as you move up warm rock that feels like an extension of your body.

We sat quietly looking down through trees on the hillside high above the town of Calpe as the hot sun dropped into the sparkling Mediterranean. Neil grinned, slowly smoking one of his little roll-up cigarettes mostly made from scavenged tobacco – he was always too broke to buy Marlboros or Embassy.

We were an unusual pair of climbing partners. He was half my age – I probably looked like an old Merchant City mincer out with his bumboy. Aw, fuck it, who cares? Although he could climb things that I couldn't get up with a ladder, we got on well.

It was as simple as that. When you are playing in a band, this kind of thing might happen occasionally with one or two other musicians, like John Gilston, and you learn not to analyse it, just let it happen. We were glowing; we'd just finished a perfect day's climbing. And I *knew* this feeling.

We knew we were both experiencing the same thing, the same total release. Murray had written about this heightened state of awareness as 'an occasional reward of hard climbs, it is a gift of the gods; if looked for it never happens'. We realised exactly what he was talking about.

'This is brilliant, Neil. This calmness. This space. This is what really matters. When you can reach out and touch the horizon and you know you are part of it. When you feel there is no time and all the time there ever was. This is life, the *real* life; all that work back home is just what we have to do to earn money. When I'm back in Glasgow and getting stressed, this is what I'll remember and come right back to.'

I *knew* this feeling.

Neil smiled and let the smoke drift from his mouth. 'Man, this is what I used to take Ecstasy for. To get this high. To get this feeling. In fact, drugs never got me even close to being this high. It's just so fucking natural.'

The thinking seems to be that spiritual enlightenment is a difficult objective only achievable, if at all, through years of commitment, denial and hard discipline. Does that mean that all of us, all working people in the West, are doomed? I mean, can you see any responsible person from Edinburgh, Glasgow or London in their right mind making a 1,000-mile pilgrimage in the buff, prostrating themselves every few steps, begging for scraps to stay alive? Or walking stiffly round and round the same mountain every day for four years? Who's got time for that?

There are businesses to run, kids to feed; hospitals that need doctors to be there, not disappearing off on some major life quest to discover their inner self. Or whatever. In the East, it might be possible to sit in a cave or wander the country for years seeking the 'truth', but in our part of the world we have to find answers more quickly and simply. We have to find a way of reconciling the insanity all around us with some sense that will allow us to go from day to day without ending up in an asylum. I sat on the cliff wondering if an enlightened state of existence is easier to achieve than we think.

Perhaps it is like climbing – it is all about a sense of balance. Perhaps it is not about compulsive ownership, but neither denial; a balance between what we need to do and what we can be. Perhaps enlightenment grows in the appreciation of simple things, in places like mountains. What was it Murray said? 'On mountains it is that spiritual part that we unconsciously develop.' When the selfish landowner stands in front of us with his snarling dogs, or the vandal petulantly hacks down life-saving guide poles, perhaps they are attempting to deny us far more than access to our hills. They are denying us access to the soul of Scotland, to ourselves. To enlightenment.

If there is such a state, then surely it must be our natural state of being? Perhaps it is not a condition to be aspired to, as though it comes from somewhere else, but one that we recover, one that we recall. It is not some new consciousness, as though it is outside, separate from us, but is simply the way we can be, as spiritual beings, mindful of the present moment. The physical demands of the body, of living, swamp us, deflecting attention, and we forget who we are and where we have been. We are caught between seeking pleasure and being unable to embrace it because we cannot leave behind the pain of previous times.

Perhaps recovering this awareness may not be difficult; it is maintaining it in this world that is the hard part, even if you wanted to – not much gets done if you are floating in a state of serenity. It is a question of balance. When we stare to the west, wondering if what we are seeking is over there, if calmness of soul is just beyond the next horizon, it is a mirage; we can never find it there. *There are no shortcuts* because it is here already;

there is nowhere we are going to. *We are here, now.* We just don't realise it.

We sat quietly on the Spanish cliff, our bodies streaked with sweat and climbing chalk, clothes dirty from the dust and rock and ropes, watching lights coming on in the village far below, calm in the warm air of dusk, the settling.

And I *knew* this feeling.

27

THE CIRCLE IS UNBROKEN

Glencoe reincarnation

I WAS IN A CHEERY MOOD. PRETTY DAMN CHEERY. I HAD BEEN WORKING towards this moment for a long time, almost half my life, in fact. I hadn't felt this good since I was young and gigging. No more Monday mornings, no more traffic jams. I'd sold the business.

And it felt so good.

At last, I'd completed all the loose ends, signed the final bits of paper, given the taxman his wad, paid the lawyers, and for once didn't grudge a penny. The new owners very kindly asked me to stay on as their Scottish area manager, but it was time to move on. I quietly left the building for the last time, went home and, for some unknown reason, spent the next hour or so cutting the garden hedge – I think I was in a state of shock. Then I went for a walk up Dumgoyne Hill. Sitting with my back against the concrete trig point at the top, I looked across the countryside to the vast sprawl of Glasgow and heaved a long sigh of relief as years of responsibility dropped from my shoulders. *I'm free.*

Over the next six months or so, friends repeatedly told me I'd soon be bored out my mind; that at only 52, I was far too young to retire, that I'd miss the daily buzz, the excitement. In Scotland, you don't need to look very far for an adrenalin rush. I went skiing.

It was one of those days when the sky was so blue you could almost see the darkening of outer space, and once you were above Rannoch Moor, the curve of the earth. The autumn gales had finally blown themselves out, the howling rain stopped, the wailing trees lulled themselves to sleep and at last Scotland was waking up below a golden sunrise, quiet and still.

It was just after dawn and I was driving to Glen Coe. Every so often, a bitter Arctic wind meets moist airflow from the Atlantic and dumps loads of perfect snow. For a day or so, the slopes are white and squeak beneath your skis, just like in Courmayeur. As I drove north, glugging down a large cup of strong coffee to jump-start my heart, the roads were clear, alpenglow brushing the top of Ben Lomond like an Olympic torch.

Loch Lomond seemed to be yawning, soft mist rising to meet the warmth of the sun. I was free; no more tedious meetings talking about removals and the cost of diesel, no more sales calls, no more crawling around customers' attics trying to figure out how many boxes we would need to pack away their lifelong collections of junk. Best of all, no more slavering, frothing-at-the-mouth Rottweilers leaping at my nuts. *They won't harm you; they're just being friendly.* Aye, right.

It used to take years to progress beyond even the most basic level in skiing. It was elitist. Then snowboarding farted in its face. You could learn to snowboard in a week – who the hell wanted those long, stiff, cold, thin planks of wood? Suddenly the ski slopes were packed with young, attractive boarders. Many of them did things traditional skiers had never dreamed of; they wore cool clothes in laid-back colours and laughed at one-piece Day-Glo quilted ski suits, especially the huge arses crammed into straining, tight pants. They plugged themselves into Walkmans and MP3s, listened to them loud. Some of them even sat on the pistes, chilling, before hurtling up and over a large mound of snow into a perfectly controlled back flip, catching some serious air, gripping it and ripping it. They didn't give a shit about pole-planting or so-called black runs, parallel turns and all that crap, and there was no way they were ever going to wear those ridiculous *Star Wars* storm-trooper boots that made people walk like pigeons with hernias. It's amazing what they can do on what looks like little more than a baker's tray. Alex has offered to teach me to board and I'd love to try, but generally speaking it is a bad idea to take it up when you have a metal plate and four screws in your neck holding your spine together. Which I have. Creak.

The ski manufacturers realised what was happening and completely redesigned their products before it was too late. They brought out short skis which made it easier to turn. If you can do that, you can stop. When you know you can stop, you soon gain confidence. They called them carvers because anyone could quickly learn how to slice huge turns in the snow. Skis that almost skied by themselves; in good snow, all you had to do was stand in them, alternate pressure on your feet and they turned as if on rails. Big toe, wee toe. How hard is that? Even I could do it.

It was like replacing an old crash gearbox with a creamy smooth Mercedes automatic. Suddenly skiing was fun and easy to learn. The new skis were so successful that a new generation of kids, who might have been doomed to computer games, took it up when they found you could do somersaults, tricks and, if you were crazy enough, even leap off small cliffs in them. In America, 'terrain parks' were built in all the major snow resorts for boarders and crazy skiers who wanted to do more than slide down nice corrugated pistes.

I'm a hopeless skier, but I love it. Oh, sure, I've done the jumps, but never intentionally: I just couldn't stop myself until it was too late. Alex had been working very hard building up Summits' website and he took me on a manufacturers' ski-test week in Italy to try out the next year's models. He reckoned I was the ideal person to test beginner-level skis designed for people who want to learn, but can only manage the occasional week abroad with the kids – an important area of his business. I had also stayed away from *the drink* since New Zealand and Alex knew I could save my ration of the sponsors' complimentary top-notch champagne for him. Hey, I have my uses.

I didn't realise I would be surrounded by ex-Olympic racers and pro testers who were snapping into the latest electronically modified computer-designed models, but what the hell. Some American skis even have microchips in them to instantly soften and harden the ski according to how icy the runs are. I think that we can safely say that even by the strictest of tests this represents real progress.

Me . . . I picked skis that had great colours.

Access to the manufacturers' stalls was by special pass and, yes, I did let it nonchalantly flutter at my neck. Two young board dudes saw it, checked out the Day-Glo skis on my feet and concluded that the specky fart who was sharing the ski lift with them must be one of the racing veterans brought in by Salomon or Rossignol to check the railing power of their prototypes. When I fell on my arse trying to get out of the chair, they wet themselves. *Aw, bollocks.* Served me right. It was a good week.

In Scotland, it was so still I couldn't hear my tyres on the road. The thermometer said it was minus eight outside, even in the early morning sun. Near Glen Coe there is a calm stretch of water – I think it's called Loch Bà – and I stopped for a while. It was so beautiful: completely frozen with a bluish-white colour that made it look like frozen milk. The air was as clean and crisp as a 1950s hospital bed.

Scotland's ski resorts have a hard time of it. They are labours of love. Nothing can be as uncertain as the forthcoming season in Scotland. How the owners of Glencoe, Glenshee and The Lecht get any sleep is something I can't imagine. Their bank managers must be saints or fools, or have been photographed in black stockings and suspenders at some fetish party in Bearsden. Yeah, snow comes, it always does, but then so too come the winds, ripping the snow off the slopes, dumping it over the roads, blocking them, or making the lifts sway so much they have to be closed. Yet still they open whenever they can and we should be proud that they do. The owners of these resorts clearly weren't listening at business school or they would have closed long ago. They should be knighted.

When an old Eskimo knows his time has come, which, by yet-to-be-accepted medical thinking, is when every pee hurts and on a good day takes half an hour, he shrugs his shoulders, calmly welcomes his destiny and walks far out on the ice with the wind at his back until he is exhausted, then simply turns round. He could save himself the trouble by coming to Glenshee and catching the lift to the top of the Cairnwell on a windy day. The windchill in Scotland can be ferocious. It is like paint-stripper on raw flesh.

Everyone who has ever skied or boarded in Scotland knows this, but it is such a delight to be able to ski in the beauty of the Highlands that the slopes attract thousands at weekends when conditions would empty any Italian or French resort. They somehow forget the last time when they only just escaped hypothermia and had to pole *downhill* against the wind to get back to the car. The snow is often like corrugated concrete, but when it is good, it is magical. If you ever get to see a purple sunset turning the white tops of the mysterious Cairngorms crimson, you'll never forget it. And it is great training – if you can ski in Scotland, you can ski anywhere. It's just a pity about the coffee.

In Italy or Spain, you can stop at any tiny little bar, small village café or mountain *refugio* and for a lousy euro buy a wonderful cup of espresso with that fawn, creamy surface. It's easy to make. Scotland has come a long way in recent years – some hotshot sales rep must be earning a fortune selling proper espresso machines; there are now many havens where it is possible to buy a really good cup of Segafredo. One of the best is the 'Shag Inn', a welcoming hostelry in which to dry out after wading off a Munro in the pouring rain. It is in a secluded spot within easy reach of Glasgow and each bedroom has its own sauna. Inside, the luxurious hotel is usually deserted, although the large car park is crammed full with Jaguars, Mercs and BMWs. If you carefully watch the side exit which leads to the car park, every so often you will see peeping round the door the darting eyes and heavy jowls of company directors, accountants or lawyers, their faces flushed pink from steam and Viagra. Then they make a run for it, pushing their heads down into their chests and pulling their briefcases up to hide their faces as they rush their young female friends into their cars and drive them back to the city. As they make their escape, desperate not to be noticed by anyone who might know their wives, it never seems to dawn on them that their personalised number plates are as recognisable as advertising posters.

Unfortunately, Glencoe Ski Centre's coffee was provided courtesy of an instant-coffee machine, the sort that offers 'frothy Kappachino'. I like my cappuccino fast, as do most skiers, but it doesn't have to be *that* fast. Oh well, the slopes make up for it.

That day Glen Coe was superb; Scotland's mountains make this place so special. They have an aura, an atmosphere of something timeless; when you look down on Rannoch Moor stretching for miles over to the cone of Schiehallion, you would not be surprised to see a dinosaur lift his head for a moment in the brief warmth of the winter sun, open one eye then settle back down to its hibernation. There must be all sorts of prehistoric bones deep in the peat.

I took the chairlift up the hill, looking down into the tumbling waterfall the Lecturer and I had been so careful to avoid all those years ago. She'd since found her man – a nice millionaire who didn't like Elvis or *Star Trek*, with a warm city apartment and a country cottage with a massive garden for the weekends; she's very happy. I worked my way up the hill, gripping the metal ski-tow with my hands, legs, teeth – anything – and trying not to fall as it dragged me almost to the top of the mountain, then I plodded up the short distance to the summit, a Munro called Meall a' Bhuiridh (Gaelic for 'peak of the mad boarders, dude'). A few other people stood gasping at the glorious views, with expressions like children at Christmas let loose in a toy warehouse and told to help themselves. We knew we were experiencing the most perfect day of the winter. Tomorrow, the runs would harden, perhaps there might be winds that would rip the snow into the air, exposing rocks like dark teeth. But today . . .

I clamped on my short, broad skis, so light they can be carried in a rucksack – they are designed so that you can climb mountains then ski back down again. I slipped on my headphones, switched on my iPod, turned up the volume to full and started to slide down from the top, grinning as I picked up speed, curving from side to side, the skis gripping the fresh, firm snow, turning as if on rails, throwing up streams of dry powder-snow like icing sugar. I couldn't imagine anywhere in the world with skiing like this, with this view. What a brilliant thing to do with a mountain.

I swooped downhill, so happy to be in this primeval, prehistoric land, looking out onto a landscape essentially unchanged for thousands of years. I felt as if I was visiting Scotland long before the first human breath, in the calm after the volcanoes erupted and lightning had licked the seas. The skis were like flying machines that let me soar over the peaks and dip into the glens, in this vast white playground, below the blue sky and the towering black rock of the Bookle, which seemed so close you could touch it. And on my headphones, Robin Williamson's haunting voice:

> Now over the skyline, I see you travelling;
> Brothers from all time
> Gathering here

Then, as he sang his masterpiece 'Maya', I realised I have been listening to it for 30 years and still can hardly grasp the meaning of half of it. Until that day, when somehow it made sense as I rode the snow from the top of the mountain all the way down to the glen.

> Small waves and thunder be my pillow . . .
> And every place shall be my native home

No one else in this world could compose something like 'Maya'. No one else has the mind of Robin, so full of the most exquisite imagery it must drive him close to insanity.

> All this world is but a play
> Be thou the joyful player

I am sure he had first written those words long ago in a play. Then later, in other lives, he had been a poet drinking hemlock, or a broken-hearted writer on a South Sea island. The being who wrote these words is an old soul, visiting again, now a musician, weaving words in song.

As I looked across Rannoch Moor and around the mountains circling far in all directions, I realised that Scotland is not its big cities – Edinburgh, Glasgow, Aberdeen or Dundee; the cities are triumphs of mankind in a harsh, empty land; the architects and engineers who built them saviours of a brave race fighting for survival in a merciless climate. The cities are the pulse, the driving energy, the muscle and brain, but the soul of Scotland is the vast calm, the towering peaks, sighing pines, deep lochs and gentle streams. In not knowing their soul, the cities will be lost, trapped in an endless cycle of decay, tortured by violence and despair.

As I reached the foot of the hill, I breathed deeply, trying to imprint for ever the image in front of me, the serenity of Scotland, poised, glowing quietly in the snow and the sunshine, a masterpiece of geological landscaping, the exquisite balance of mountains and glens. A universal kindness must have created this perfection and Robin's song was born of it.

All this world is but a play . . .

I opened the door of my car and eased off my ski boots – always a delight. Ahh . . . I dropped them on the floor and slipped my feet into something comfortable. I headed to Tyndrum for coffee and as I drove, the sky behind the hills exploded in the last colours of the day. I watched in silence as a falling star lit up the purple sky, then grinned when Ben Lui, Scotland's Matterhorn, swung into view, glowing in the light of the full moon. What a place. I glanced at my feet and suddenly realised I was wearing sandals. With socks.

ACKNOWLEDGEMENTS

PROBABLY BECAUSE I AM BOTH A MUSICIAN AND A WRITER, I HAVE HUNDREDS
of words and phrases from songs dancing in my head; they have
been part of my life since that first fantastic moment when I
switched on the radio and heard the Stones and The Beatles. In
any given situation, an apt song line will spring to mind. I love
it. Most authors have an array of quotes to call on from great
books whenever there is a slight lull in the conversation; all rock
guitarists have a handy repertoire of 'licks' and riffs they play
whenever the mood takes them – my mind is full of a strange
mixture of both. I feel very lucky.

It was my original intention to use many of these at
appropriate points in the book, especially as chapter headings.
But I reckoned without showbiz lawyers. It is interesting that
they expect total artistic freedom for their clients, and I
completely agree with them, but chilling to notice that they
might not be so willing to extend the same privilege to anyone
else. In the section where I talk about hillwalking with my
children, I was going to use a line from a Kinks song thanking

my sons for the days they gave me and how I won't forget a single one. When I played with Powerhouse many years ago, we did a gig with The Kinks and I met Ray Davies a couple of times. He is a very nice guy and I am sure he would never object to my using the exact line from his song. However, I discovered a few weeks prior to the book being printed that copyright law prohibits this without the written consent of the artist. I am sure Ray has more pressing demands on his time.

In the paragraph where I describe watching a fantastic thunderstorm in Glen Sheil, I mention that I was listening to Jimi, whose music fits so well with these vast elemental storms. I was lucky enough to meet Jimi, well, sort of – OK, I got to shake his hand in Argyle Street when he played in Glasgow – but feel sure from people who did know him that he would never object to any unknown admiring author mentioning a few words from one or two of his songs. When I contacted the copyright holders in Seattle, I was told that I could not refer to kissing the sky without sending them a synopsis of the book, the chapter concerned, details of the print run, confirmation that the book would not deal with certain subjects they deem to be unsuitable (sex being one of them) and, of course, pay them a fee of anything from $200 upwards. I would have to submit my initial application to the giant Sony Corporation in the UK and it would eventually be passed through the American office for their consideration. I would have to wait for approval. This might take some time.

Hell, I would never steal anyone's work or attempt to pass off famous lines as my own. I mean, come on, guys, these are really well-known songs; we've been listening to them for almost half a century. All I wanted was to share with fellow music lovers some of the joy that rock music has given me, especially on mountains, perhaps compare notes. Isn't that what music and freedom are all about? This book is the work of a fan, a lifelong enthusiast; it is certainly not about money. Even if it were to be a runaway bestseller, I doubt I'd earn more than 10p for every hour I spent writing it and I am perfectly happy about that. It is a labour of love; to see this in print is the realisation of a dream.

So, I am sorry I didn't have time to indulge the powershake-guzzling paralegals by filling out endless reams of forms when there was a simple compromise. I could have used the words, *pardon me, while I embrace the sky*, but most people would think I had finally gone insane.

Fortunately, song titles are exempt from copyright law, therefore I have used them instead of the words we all know and love so much. I am sure you can fill in the blanks. The other 'out' is where I have referred to a few songs from the point of view of comparison and review, also permitted by the thought-police.

Having ranted thus, I would like to acknowledge the following artists/copyright holders for the truly great music they have given us; our lives would be far less wonderful without it: Small Faces, Led Zeppelin, Eric Clapton, Cream, Johnny Nash, Steve Earle, The Kinks, Aerosmith, Cat Stevens, Mike Heron, Richard Thomson, Marc Bolan, Bob Dylan, the Rolling Stones, Manic Street Preachers, Dobie Gray, U2, Boston, Robin Williamson, Little Feat, David Bowie, ZZ Top, Joni Mitchell, Nat King Cole, Frank Sinatra, The Beautiful South, Trent Reznor, Notorious BIG, Tenacious D, The Who, Slim Harpo, Frank Zappa and Jimi Hendrix. I sincerely apologise for any omissions or inaccuracies and will endeavour to correct future editions.